Companion to the
Revised Common Lectionary

4. All Age Worship Year C

Joyce Barrass

Companion to the Revised Common Lectionary

4. All Age Worship Year C

EPWORTH PRESS

0 7162 0541 6

*First Published 2000
by Epworth Press
20 Ivatt Way
Peterborough, PE3 7PG*

*Typeset by Regent Typesetting, London
Printed and bound in Great Britain by
Biddles Ltd, Guildford and King's Lynn*

Contents

This book is dedicated to my mum, Margaret,
and to Jack, Jathni and my dear friends whose love
and support mean more to me than they will know.

ALL AGE WORSHIP YEAR C

FIRST SUNDAY OF ADVENT

Jeremiah 33.14–16; Psalm 25.1–10; I Thessalonians 3.9–13;
Luke 21.25–36

SIGNS AND SHOOTS

Presentation

*Illustration: Display pictures that encourage the congregation to
guess 'what happens next'. Examples might be someone carrying too
much heavy shopping, about to drop everything, or a strong wind
blowing in a street, about to blow away hats, umbrellas, etc. The
final image would be of a bud, ready to burst into blossom. What
signs do we look for to warn us that things are about to happen?
When we see the red or green man at a pelican crossing, we get
ready to cross the road. When we see signs of what God is doing in
the world, we need to be taking note and ready to join in.*

(1) Call to Worship

Psalm 25.4–5; or the following:

To you, O Lord, I lift up my soul:
My God, I put my trust in you.
Let me not be humiliated, nor my enemies get the better of me:
My God, I put my trust in you.
Let nobody who looks to you be put to shame:
My God, I put my trust in you.

(2) Meditation

*Suitable music could be played during this meditation, especially a
piece that builds to a climax from a quiet beginning!*

All around us, signs and promises,
Whispers of warning from a voice that cares;
We see the horizon blossoming into expectant colours,
Through the dawn frosts the fires of orange, gold and scarlet,
And we prepare our eyes to see the sun rising, breaking free from
    the silent earth.
When we hear the breakfast bacon sizzling and our noses twitch
    with the delicious smell
Of warm bread toasting, we get ready to enjoy the first meal of the
    day.

Walking along to school over the railway, our ears hear the
warning bells ringing,
Our eyes can see the red lights warning that a train is on the way to
the crossing.
All around us, signs and promises.
Give us open hearts and minds to take notice of the clues you give
That you are in control, and you are preparing us to join your
dance.

(3) Prayer of Adoration

God, you promised through Jeremiah, a righteous branch springing
from David's line.
Right from the first you planned for us the joy that Jesus would
bring;
And this is the name you gave to the branch:
The Lord is our righteousness.
God, you sent your Son Jesus, to bring with him justice,
To bring righteousness to the land.
And this is the name you gave to the branch:
The Lord is our righteousness.
God, you gave your people signs that they would be saved,
And this is the name you gave to the branch:
The Lord is our righteousness.
God, we adore you, for keeping your promises;
Jesus, the branch of David's line, came to reveal your purposes,
And this is the name you gave to the branch:
The Lord is our righteousness.

(4) Prayer of Confession

We are sorry, Compassionate God, for not listening when you want
to talk to us;
We sometimes go on in our own ways and miss the warning signs;
We head into trouble because we don't pay attention to you.
We are sorry for not looking at your signs in creation;
You show us all the beauty of sun and moon, stunning stars and
mysterious planets,
But we forget to look, and forget to say 'Thank you'.
We are sorry for not taking notice,
When people are hurting, crying our for help, longing for love;
You tell us: 'Look out!' but we keep on looking in at ourselves.
Silence

God who cares, we ask for your forgiveness for not getting ready.
Help us now to listen and watch for your loving Word waking up
the world.

(5) Prayer of Petition

Among the frightened and the ones who frighten others:
**May we abound with love for others as we abound in love for
you.**
Among those who feel they have no one to guide them and the
ones who lead others astray:
**May we abound with love for others as we abound in love for
you.**
Among those who feel nothing will ever change and those who are
scared it will:
**May we abound with love for others as we abound in love for
you.**

(6) Prayer of Dismissal

Based on I Thessalonians 3.13

May God so strengthen our hearts in holiness that we may be
blameless before our God and Father at the coming of our Lord Jesus
Christ.

SECOND SUNDAY OF ADVENT

Baruch 5.1–9 or Malachi 3.1–4; Luke 1.68–79; Philippians 1.3–11;
Luke 3.1–6

ROBING AND READINESS

Presentation

*Illustration: A short obstacle course made from stacked books,
chairs etc. in the aisle or at the front of the church. Someone
negotiates this blindfolded, with help and encouragement from the
congregation. The obstacles are then cleared away, making the trip
up the aisle much safer and smoother! How did the congregation
help to guide the 'traveller' on the way? Did it feel easier and safer
when the way was made free from obstacles? Do we put any
obstacles in the way of those trying to follow God's path? How can
we help to 'make his paths straight' for others?*

(7) Call to Worship

Malachi 3.1 or Luke 3.4–6

(8) Prayer of Adoration

Advent Lord, we want to sing the song of joy to you,
That sang in the heart of Zechariah; filled with the Holy Spirit,
He saw the promise of salvation coming true, as we do now in
     Jesus.
Praise be to the Lord, the God of Israel:
Because he has come to his people and set them free.

Advent Lord, we want to sing out your praises,
That you set us free to worship you without fear, holy and
     righteous in your sight
All the days of our life.
Praise be to the Lord, the God of Israel:
Because he has come to his people and set them free.

Advent Lord, you set us free from all that binds us,
You bring us your healing and shalom, calling us to prepare your
     way.
Praise be to the Lord, the God of Israel:
Because he has come to his people and set them free.

(9) Prayer of Confession

In the tender compassion of our God, the dawn from on high shall
   break on us
To shine on those who dwell in darkness and the shadow of death,
And to guide our feet into the way of peace.
Lord Jesus, we confess now all the times we have chosen darkness
   to hide from your light.
We say sorry for cruel words and actions chosen instead of kind
   ones.
And as we say sorry, we ask for your light to guide our feet into the
   way of your peace.

(10) Prayer of Thanksgiving

Thank you, God, that you are the light that guides our feet:
That you are the one who makes the crooked straight,
That you are the one who has come to set us free.
Thank you, God, for the ones who help us to walk on your path
   safely:
For teachers, and people who help us to cross the road,
For roadsweepers, coastguards and rescue teams.
Thank you, Lord, for Jesus, our guide and our pathway this Advent.

(11) Prayer of Petition

Wherever we find danger, help us to be brave and wise:
Guide our feet into the way of peace.
Wherever we find fighting and quarrelling, help us to be bridge-
   builders:
Guide our feet into the way of peace.
Wherever we find hunger and hopelessness, help us to bring hope
   in action:
Guide our feet into the way of peace.
Wherever we find wounds and wandering, help us to point the way
   home to healing:
Guide our feet into the way of peace.

(12) Prayer of Dedication

Based on Philippians 1.3–11

Giving God, we can be confident of this, that you, who have begun a good work in us, will bring it to completion until the day of Jesus Christ. May we rejoice and thank you for all those who walk your path with us, as we hold one another in our hearts. This is our prayer, that our love may abound more and more in knowledge and depth of insight, to the glory and praise of God.

(13) Prayer of Dismissal

Based on Baruch 5.1

Go now; take off the garment of your sorrow, and put on forever the beauty of the glory from God; for God has ordered that every high mountain and the everlasting hills be made low, so that his people may walk safely in the glory of God. **We go, to walk in his way.**

THIRD SUNDAY OF ADVENT

Zephaniah 3.14–20; Isaiah 12.2–6; Philippians 4.4–7; Luke 3.7–18

RESTORED AND REJOICING

Presentation
Illustration: The Old Testament and Epistle passages have rejoicing as a theme. Discuss: what makes us want to rejoice and give thanks to God? Personal objects or photographs which remind us about such things might be shared. Then show pictures where reasons to rejoice are less obvious. Do we rejoice 'always'? Talk about a cartoon of a character clearly bandaged, but with the caption 'Alleluia anyway!' If we bring even the disappointments to God, we are promised 'the peace of God, which passes all understanding'.

(14) Call to Worship

Isaiah 12.2–3; or the following:

Sing to the Lord, for he has done glorious things:
Let this be known to all the world!
Shout aloud and sing for joy, people of Zion:
For great is the Holy One of Israel among us!

(15) Prayer of Adoration

Lord God, astonishing Creator,
We rejoice in all your love has made, from the furthest glittering
    galaxy,
To the most minute and mystifying molecules right under our
    noses;
From the oceans lapping around the earth to the information
    circling on the Internet quicker than lightning!
Rejoice in the Lord, always:
Again I say: Rejoice!

Lord God, known to us in Jesus, we rejoice to know a friend so
    wonderful,
Who will take our worries and fears and share them,
Who will take our pains and puzzlement and heal them.
Rejoice in the Lord, always:
Again I say: Rejoice!

Lord God, Holy Spirit,
We rejoice in your free cartwheeling dance that unites us, guides us
    and lights up our lives!
Rejoice in the Lord, always:
Again I say: Rejoice!

(16) Prayer of Confession

We have so much, we sometimes forget to share it.
We know so many things, we sometimes boast about it.
We need so much, we sometimes forget to ask you for it.
We get bored so easily, we sometimes forget to let you excite us.
God who forgives, you entrust so much to us, we sometimes forget
    to thank you for it.
We hear your gentle word of grace, telling us all our sins are
    forgiven.
Now may we let such gentleness as you show us, be known to
    everyone.

(17) Prayer of Thanksgiving

Read Philippians 4.4–7

For people who show us how to sing when they are suffering:
We thank you, Advent Lord.
For people who show us how to skip when the road seems lonely:
We thank you, Advent Lord.
For people who show us how to relax when the world seems too
    hectic:
We thank you, Advent Lord.
For people who show us how to rejoice in the peace that Jesus
    gives us:
We thank you, Advent Lord.

(18) Meditation

The river flows at the Baptist's feet; I sway with the crush of the
    crowd.
I want to feel the cool water, renewing me, restoring me to joy.
But his eyes bore through me: can he see how smug I feel?
I want to plunge in, but I need to be ready.
He says: 'Bear fruits worthy of repentance.'
He can see my two coats and the naked one beside me.
He can see my purse bulging and this stranger who has no money.

He can hear the echo of threats still on my tongue and the one I
   wounded.
'Teacher, what should I do?'
He tells of the One who comes to baptize with pure fire,
Burning away my hard heart, winnowing away my stubbornness.
Take my extra coat, my hoarded gold, my power games;
Roll them under the water that closes over my head,
In ripples of relief and rejoicing.

(19) Prayer of Dedication

Surely God is my salvation; I will trust and not be afraid.
Take what we are, restored to you rejoicing.
Take what we have, gifts generously poured from your heart.
Take what we will be, drawing pure water from wells of salvation.
Surely God is my salvation; I will trust and not be afraid.

(20) Prayer of Dismissal

Philippians 4.7

FOURTH SUNDAY OF ADVENT

Micah 5.2–5a; Luke 1.47–55 or Psalm 80.1–7; Hebrews 10.5–10;
Luke 1.39–45 (46–55)

TURNING THE WORLD UPSIDE DOWN!

Presentation

*Illustration: Invite some members of the congregation to line up in
order of height, age etc. Begin to offer a prize to the winner (tallest,
oldest) then suddenly change the criterion and make the smallest
or youngest the winner instead. Read 'The Magnificat'; invite
discussion about how the rich or powerful may have felt they were
'winning' with God. He turns the world's values upside down. Do we
judge success by power, fastest cars, biggest houses (or churches!)?
Jesus came to bring a new justice.*

(21) Call to Worship

Read Micah 5. 2–5a

(22) Prayer of Adoration

God of Advent joy, we adore you for turning this world upside
    down!
You take no notice of the powerful, the loud or the showy.
You were born in a tiny town in a humble manger bed.
My soul proclaims the greatness of the Lord:
My spirit rejoices in God my Saviour.

God of the humble and the ordinary,
We adore you for caring about the things we often overlook,
For choosing the powerless and the insignificant to reveal God's
    love to all.
My soul proclaims the greatness of the Lord:
My spirit rejoices in God my Saviour.

God of patience and promises,
You came to earth to burst the bubble of those who puff themselves
    up,
To lift up the lowly and fill the hungry with good things.
My soul proclaims the greatness of the Lord:
My spirit rejoices in God my Saviour.

(23) Prayer of Confession

Read Hebrews 10.5–10

God, when we try to impress you, with technicolour offerings and
    widescreen sacrifices,
When we make a lot of noise about how much we have done for
    you,
When we turn up the volume to drown out your quiet call:
Forgive us. *Silence*
Lord, you sweep up all the ashes of our show and shouting from
    the altar;
You let us say the words you want to hear instead:
'Here I am, O Lord, we have come to do your will, O God.'
We rise forgiven; restored to the arms that hold us in love without
    limit.

(24) Prayer of Dedication

God of surprises, you make us do handstands
So that the wrong values we cram in our pockets
Simply fall out with a bump as you turn the world upside down.
If we imagine our offerings come out of our own goodness,
You twirl round our microscope, making a telescope,
Sweeping wider and wiser, until we see clearly,
That these gifts are your gifts, our hands, your hands.
Make us dizzy, Lord, to see things your way around.

(25) Prayer of Dismissal

Jesus is coming into our world: **to turn our world around**.
Jesus is coming into our lives: **to turn our lives around.**
Jesus is coming into our hearts: **to turn our hearts around.**
May we make him welcome!

CHRISTMAS DAY

Isaiah 52.7–10; Psalm 98; Hebrews 1.1–4 (5–12); John 1.1–14

THE WORD BECOMES FLESH

Presentation

Illustration: Show a variety of Christmas decorations, figures, models etc. both made up complete and as written instructions and diagrams only. Get children to join in with the making. Draw out the difference between written word or flat diagram and the 3D finished article. Was it as easy to picture the models on paper? Jesus makes the Word of God come alive for us. He helps us to understand God's purposes, by becoming human. How can we make the Good News 'come alive' for people we meet?

(26) Call to Worship

Isaiah 52.7 or John 1.14

(27) Prayer of Adoration

Presents may be shown and the leader may draw out if these are what the recipients have always wanted, or did they come as a surprise? Jesus was a bit of both! Leading into . . .

Lord, on the day of your coming, we can hardly contain our joy.
You are the best gift, the one the world has been waiting for since the beginning.
You unwrapped yourself as the promise of God, giving flesh and blood to dreams and hopes;
The world held its breath for your birth; we join in now with the cries of joy and welcome.
You are the best gift, long awaited but still coming to surprise us.
The world is so used to darkness, your light wakes us up with its radiance.
Gift of the Father, you are life, the life that is light to all people.
You have given us a new song to sing,
For God has done marvellous things.

(28) Prayer of Thanksgiving

Jesus, gift of glory, we thank God that you have come to bring
    good news of salvation.
Let the rivers clap their hands:
Let the hills ring out with joy before the Lord.
Jesus, gift of grace, we thank God that you have come to make the
    Word flesh.
Let the rivers clap their hands:
Let the hills ring out with joy before the Lord.
Jesus, gift of radiance, we thank God that the darkness will never
    put out your light.
Let the rivers clap their hands:
Let the hills ring out with joy before the Lord.

(29) Prayer of Petition

God who comes as living light, may we run with the light to bring
    your glow of love into the darkest corners.
God who comes as the Word made flesh, may we do more than
    mutter about the Good News, but live it among those who long
    to meet you face to face.
God who comes as the gift of love to a waiting world, may we keep
    nobody waiting as we share your gift with those who hunger and
    thirst for your Christmas love.
Lord, may we not throw you away with the trimmings and
    wrappers, but celebrate your birth with the joy that never fades
    or fails us.

(30) Prayer of Dedication

Come with us as we carry your light to the damaged and
disheartened ones:
And all the ends of the earth shall see the salvation of our God.
Come with us as we carry your hope to the weeping and weary ones:
And all the ends of the earth shall see the salvation of our God.
Come with us as we carry your peace to the uneasy and the bitter
    ones:
And all the ends of the earth shall see the salvation of our God.
Come with us as on the mountains, in streets and homes, beautiful
    feet of the messenger bring the good news, announcing your
    saving love:
Our God reigns.

(31) Prayer of Dismissal

Go to share the glory of the word made flesh:
we go to share his glory.
Go to share the grace of the one who lives among us:
we go to share his grace.
Go to share the truth of the Father's only son:
we go to share his truth.

FIRST SUNDAY OF CHRISTMAS

I Samuel 2.18–20,26; Psalm 148; Colossians 3.12–17; Luke 2.41–52

GIFT AND GROWTH

Presentation

Illustration: Play hide and seek with a person or item. What did it feel like to be searched for? Have we lost sight of a parent or child temporarily while shopping? Did we panic? Or wonder what all the fuss was about? Jesus and Samuel both felt at home in the temple. We don't feel lost in our own surroundings. Are we relieved or surprised that God searches for us when we wander?

(32) Call to Worship

Psalm 148.1–4, with the congregation joining in each **Praise him**

(33) Prayer of Adoration

Praise the name of the Lord!
Lord God, all creation is praising your name!
Praise the name of the Lord!
Lord God, you are praised from the heights and the heavens!
All the angels delight to sing your praise!
Lord God, you are the one that sun and moon are praising,
All the stars that shine praise your holy name:
Praise the name of the Lord!

Praise the Lord from the earth, from the depths of the seas,
In wind and weather, hail and lightning, snow and fog,
Tempests and winds, mountains and high hills,
Trees and animals and birds, kings and rulers:
Praise the name of the Lord!

Young and old, men, women and children,
Let us all praise with them the name of the Lord!
Praise the name of the Lord!

(34) Prayer of Confession

God who notices, you see when nobody else realizes we are missing.
When we creep away from what we should be doing, or wander far
from those who need us,
You see, with eyes that love even when we make you weep.
You see, with a heart that loves even when we break it.
We are sorry that we make you anxious as our parent.
Not like Jesus, who was found sitting, listening and learning.
More often you find us sitting grumbling, or arguing, fighting
Or daydreaming, wasteful and worrying.
Forgive us and come and find out where we are hiding.
Silence
We are free now, to sit at your feet.
We are free now, to learn from your Word.
We are free now, from all that has burdened us.

(35) Prayer of Thanksgiving

God of opportunities, thank you for the chance to grow in you.
The chance to grow in wisdom, grace and strength, to deepen our
faith and learn your love.
Thank you for our chance to grow as children, like Samuel and
Jesus in the Temple.
Thank you for our chance to grow as adults, learning like Mary
who treasured things up in her heart.
Thank you for our chance to grow as older people, like Eli who
went on watching and wondering.
God of opportunities, thank you for the chance to grow in you.

(36) Prayer of Dedication

Patient God, waiting for us to grow, may you use us as we are;
Constant God, with us as we learn, may we listen always for your
leading;
Loving God, seeking us out of love, may the word of Christ dwell
in us richly.
Whatever we do, in word or deed, may we do everything in the
name of Jesus.

(37) Prayer of Petition

Compassionate God, clothe us: **clothe us with your compassion**.
Kind God, clothe us: **clothe us with your kindness**.
Humble God, clothe us: **clothe us with your humility.**
Merciful God, clothe us: **clothe us with your mercy.**
Patient God, clothe us: **clothe us with your patience.**
And may we bear with one another, forgiving as you forgive. In
  Jesus' name.

(39) Prayer of Dismissal

Colossians 3.15

SECOND SUNDAY OF CHRISTMAS

(if before 6 January)

Jeremiah 31.7–14 (or Ecclesiasticus 24.1–12); Psalm 147.12–20
(or Wisdom of Solomon 10.15–21); Ephesians 1.3–14;
John 1.(1–9) 10–18

A REMNANT REDEEMED

Presentation

*Illustration: Remnants and odd pieces of material. These are what
now remain from much larger carpets, curtains, clothing. (An older
member of the congregation with a well-stocked workbox may have
many treasures to share!) They may bring back memories of places
and people associated with the original items. What is the 'remnant
of Israel'? God cares about each of them, for all are a part of the
whole. Bound together by common identity as God's people, cut from
the same cloth. Never cast aside, the remnant is treasured by God,
and gathered up tenderly.*

(40) Call to Worship

Ephesians 1.3 or Jeremiah 31.10, 13b

(41) Prayer of Adoration

Wise and welcoming God, we come together to praise and adore you;
You are worthy of all worship and praise.
When we were scattered and wandering, from north to south and
    east to west,
You gathered us tenderly, consoling our weeping,
Nurturing the frail and vulnerable, attentive as a shepherd
To a broken and weary flock.
Wise and welcoming God, we praise you for all that you are.

Caring and comforting God, we come to sing of your love,
You make our lives like a watered garden,
And our sorrow you change into laughter and dance.
Our mourning becomes joy
As we skip in safety by shimmering brooks,
On straight paths where our feet will not stumble.
Caring and comforting God, we praise you for all that you are.

(42) Prayer of Confession

Silence
Through the silence of loneliness and feeling lost,
From the costly wilderness of the sin that separates,
You call us home.
Silence
Through the silence of indifference and neglect,
Over the empty wastes of our disobedience,
You call us home.
Silence
Precious Saviour, you know we have long been wandering,
Spent by shame and worn down by regrets.
We are so sorry; we are ready now to be led home by you.
Tenderly we hear you say: Be at peace, now; your sins are
   forgiven. Come home.

(43) Prayer of Thanksgiving

For blessing of God the Father,
Who chose us in Christ before the foundation of the world:
Thanks be to God.

For the plan fulfilled in Christ,
The human face of God's mysterious will:
Thanks be to God.

For the seal of the Holy Spirit,
As we hear the truth, the gospel of our salvation:
Thanks be to God.

(44) Prayer of Petition

God of refreshment, gather and renew your people.
When we feel beaten out like ashes until no spark remains,
Blow on us gently with the breath of your Spirit,
And rekindle in us your fires of faith.
Lord, refresh and rally your children,
From where time and temptation have scattered and lured us,
Bringing us back into the rainbow span of unity,
Uniquely yours and so thankful to be home!

(45) Prayer of Dedication

Take these gifts, and circle them with your grace;
Take these offerings, and build your Kingdom;
Take all we are, and use us as you deserve.

(46) Prayer of Dismissal

Let us dance out into the world, on a path where we cannot
    stumble;
Let us go singing into the world, radiant with the goodness of the
    Lord;
That all may know the God whose name is Love.

EPIPHANY (6 January)

Isaiah 60.1–6; Psalm 72.(1–7) 10–14; Ephesians 3.1–12;
Matthew 2.1–12

STARS AND DREAMS

Presentation

*Illustration: Explore the Epiphany through the senses: burn gold
coloured candles and incense sticks of frankincense and myrrh, or
put drops of these essential oils on tissues and kitchen paper. Talk
about the scent of the incense, symbolizing worship, the senses, and
priesthood as its pungent smell rises up like a bridge between earth
and heaven. The more subtle myrrh has qualities that link it with
anointing the body for burial, a facet of Jesus' life and ministry that
has its place even at the heart of this season.*

(47) Call to Worship

Isaiah 60.1–3 or the following:

Where is the child who has been born King of the Jews?
For we have seen his star in the East and have come to worship him.
Come, let us worship him!

(48) Prayer of Adoration

God we adore you, King of Kings.
Here is gold for one who is worth more than earth can afford.
Here is gold for the one who gave the costliest gift of all,
His life for our healing, who opened his Kingdom for our salvation.
God, we adore you, King of Kings.

God, we worship you, True God of True God.
Here is frankincense for our great high priest,
Who built a bridge between heaven and earth,
Breaking down all barriers, uniting and atoning.
God, we worship you, True God of True God.

God, we praise you, Lover and Friend.
Here is myrrh that speaks of sacrifice and cost beyond counting.
From cradle to cross your brave choices lead you,
Anointed for dying, and destined for rising.
God, we praise you, Lover and Friend.

(49) Prayer of Confession

They came as star chasers, following a promise,
Driven by a dream, over dunes and great distances;
At times we cannot cross the road to meet you.
Forgive us, Lord, and guide us into your presence.

They came with costly gifts to pay you homage,
Gold for the prince of Heaven, myrrh for your bittersweet anointing,
Incense for the Priest of all people.
At times our hands are grasping and our hearts empty.
Forgive us, Lord, and guide us into your presence.

As we confess our laziness, we hear a baby's cry.
As we confess our emptiness, we receive your gift of grace;
Reborn in your forgiveness, we see the star stand still,
And we kneel in silent worship as you welcome the wanderers in.
Forgive us, Lord, and guide us into your presence.

(50) Prayer of Thanksgiving

For star-led journeys, and the courage to set out;
For costly gifts of love, and open hands to give them;
For wisdom on the way, and company as we travel:
Thanks be to God!

(51) Prayer of Petition

God, may we shine with the light of your coming,
For the glory of the Lord has now risen in our lives.
Give us the courage and persistence of those wise travellers
When the way seems long, dark and uncertain.
Give us the wit and wisdom to change direction
When the world turns tricky and treacherous to catch us.

(52) Prayer of Dismissal

Go now wherever his star may lead you,
Rejoicing at every turn of the road,
Until that steady light reveals your King.

SUNDAY BETWEEN 7 AND 13 JANUARY

(First Sunday in Ordinary Time. This Sunday may be observed as Covenant Sunday)

Isaiah 43.1–7; Psalm 29; Acts 8.14–17; Luke 3.15–17, 21–22

BAPTISM OF FIRE

Presentation

Illustration: Membership ticket. What are the promises we enter into when we come to church? What are some of God's promises to us? Look at the name on the ticket. Read Isaiah 43.1. God calls us by name, and promises we are his. A covenant is a relationship, where we matter as individuals. All relationships flourish by being two-way, with responsibilities and benefits. Love binds us together.

(53) Call to Worship

Isaiah 43.1–2 or Psalm 29.1–2

(54) Meditation

Read Acts 8.14–17

Afraid to take the plunge, I teetered on the brink.
The water seemed so deep, I was trembling too much to commit
   myself;
The bank was dry and firm underfoot.
But I did it, and the waters closed over my head, eyes tight shut.
Now there is a whisper of more blessing to come,
Not water but flames of living fire, a deep infilling.
My heart is hammering like a dove in a cage.
Can there truly be more? Can I surrender?
Promise, privilege, welling and overwhelming;
I feel the quiet hands on my head. *Silence.*
A breath, a bursting galaxy of joy, a stillness,
God's Spirit flooding into my readiness,
Coming home to me as I come home.

(55) Prayer of Adoration

Covenant God, you have called us by name, into your family,
Bound by ties of love, you tell us we are yours.
Lord of belonging, we celebrate your covenant of grace;
Protector of your children:
Covenant God, we adore you.

Covenant God, you pass with us through the waters,
Through the rivers which cannot overwhelm us;
You walk with us through fire, so it might not harm us,
Protector of your children:
Covenant God, we adore you.

(56) Prayer of Thanksgiving

Thank you, God, for your transforming love in the miracle of
  creation:
The skipping calf and the cedar tree,
The pulse of new life in the frozen ground
Waiting beneath the rhythms of wind and weather.
Thank you, God, for your transforming love.
Thank you, God, for your transforming love in the miracle of Jesus:
He came humbly to the draughts and dusty rafters of obscurity,
In the corner of a stable, shrinking his radiance to the size of a
  candle,
To light up our faces and lives with wonder.
Thank you, God, for your transforming love.
Thank you, God, for your transforming love in the miracle of the
  Spirit:
The baptism that changes lives and destinies
Through the whisper of grace descending.
Thank you, God, for your transforming love.

(57) Prayer of Dedication

God of the Covenant, calling us from afar into the circle of your
  loving:
We bind ourselves to you eternally.
God of the Covenant, singing your love-song in our wayward hearts:
We bind ourselves to you eternally.
God of the Covenant, cradling our headstrong hearts in your patient
  palms:
We bind ourselves to you eternally.

(58) Prayer of dismissal

May the blessing of the Lord of All, the cherishing of the Lord of Love, the inspiration of the Lord of Life rest on us this day and refresh us forever with God's peace and power.

SUNDAY BETWEEN 14 AND 20 JANUARY

(Second Sunday in Ordinary Time. This Sunday may fall within the Octave of Prayer for Christian Unity)

Isaiah 62.1–5; Psalm 36.5–10; I Corinthians 12.1–11; John 2.1–11

WATER INTO WINE

Presentation
Illustration: Show a small glass of clean water in which you have previously placed an inverted cone of black plastic with the end cut off so it fits flush into the tumbler, making it appear, from a distance, to be filled with ink. Under cover of a handkerchief, remove the black cone, revealing the clear water. Explore how the wedding guests might have thought of Jesus as a conjuror. The 'ink' trick was an illusion. Jesus' miracle reveals his glory and promotes belief. Jesus does not act as a showman. How might Mary, the disciples, the guests, modern hearers feel about what they see?

(59) Call to Worship
Isaiah 62.1 or Psalm 36.5

(60) Prayer of Adoration

Creator God, your love reaches to the heavens, and your faithfulness to the clouds.
Your goodness and faithfulness are deep as the ocean and high as the highest peak.
With you is the fountain of life:
In your light we see light.

Creator God, your love is priceless and precious.
We find our true place under the shadow of your wings.
You provide for us feasting and drinks from the river of your delights.
With you is the fountain of life:
In your light we see light.

Creator God, the psalmist sings your glory with poems of joy.
We gather now to worship you, as we celebrate the colours,
    textures and fragrances,
The music and mystery of the universe where you place us.
With you is the fountain of life:
In your light we see light.

(61) Prayer of Confession

Listening God, we need to tell you we feel ashamed:
Of the times when we saw needs and closed our eyes;
Of the times when we saw miracles and closed our minds;
Of the times we heard weeping and closed our ears;
Of the times we had opportunities, and closed our hearts.
As you turned water into wine, turn our failures into new
    opportunities,
Turn our closed fists into open hands to bring your love to our
    neighbours.

(62) Prayer of Thanksgiving

Water for wine! **Alleluia!**
Laughter for weeping! **Alleluia!**
Faith for faltering! **Alleluia!**
Joy for sorrow! **Alleluia!**
Freedom for fetters! **Alleluia!**
Thanks to the Lord for his love that changes our world!

(63) Prayer of Dedication

Read I Corinthians 12.4–11

God of the springing, surprising Spirit, may we delight in your gifts,
and be wise to use them, without boasting or greed, for there is one
Spirit, one Lord and one God. May we use your gifts to the common
good. Wisdom, knowledge, faith, healing, miracles, prophecy,
spiritual sensitivity, tongues to proclaim and messages revealed, may
all be used in unity and harmony for the building of your Kingdom.

(64) Prayer of Dismissal

The Father has made you: **we go in the name of the Father.**
The Son has died for you: **we go in the Name of the Son.**
The Spirit has flowed into you: **we go in the Name of the Spirit.**

SUNDAY BETWEEN 21 AND 27 JANUARY

(Third Sunday in Ordinary Time. This Sunday may fall within the Octave of Prayer for Christian Unity)

Nehemiah 8.1–3, 5–6, 8–10; Psalm 19; I Corinthians 12.12–31a; Luke 4.14–21

SWEETER THAN HONEY IN THE COMB

Presentation
Illustration: Crosswords, anagrams, wordsearches, acrostics (suitable to the age and interests of the congregation!). Words can be exciting, fun, interesting, frustrating. Did we feel good about 'discovering' a word in these puzzles? Ezra's reading of the words of Moses made the people sit up and listen. It even made them want to cry! Jesus' reading of Isaiah was also like a new discovery to his listeners. What does God's word make us feel? How can we make these words come alive for new Christians and for one another?

(65) Call to Worship

The word of the Lord is sweet to our ears:
Sweeter than honey in the comb!
His laws are sure, his commands are radiant:
Sweeter than honey in the comb!
His law is perfect, reviving the soul: what he ordains is more
   precious than gold!
Sweeter than honey in the comb!
Come let us worship the Lord our God!

(66) Prayer of Adoration

The heavens declare the glory of the Lord!
Let us declare his glory in our own ways, in prayer and song, in noise and dance, in colour and craft.

The congregation could bring forward tokens of adoration, prepared beforehand, such as pictures and poems, while there could be an opportunity to worship with simple instruments, streamers etc.

One day tells its tale of God's glory to another: night to night reveals his glory, although they have no voices, their message goes out into all lands and to the ends of the world.
Let us tell the tale of God's glory with no words, in the quiet cathedral of our hearts.

An opportunity to worship God in silence and contemplation, perhaps with gentle music.

(67) Prayer of Confession

Read I Corinthians 12.12–31a

Patient God, bear with us as we confess to you. Because we are not hands, we grumble as feet, kicking against unity. Because we are not eyes, we grumble as ears, deafening ourselves to unity. Because we are jealous and shallow, we bicker and snipe, turning our backs on unity. Forgive us, Lord; you have given us so many different gifts. If we were all the same, where would the body be? As it is, there are many members, but one body. Join our hearts and hands in harmony, and make us one again where we have become disjointed and divided. Restore us to be the body of Christ, individual yet members of the whole.

(68) Prayer of Thanksgiving

God, we thank you for those who tell out your word,
Who remind us of your laws, who inspire us to read your story:
The joy of the Lord is our strength.
We thank you for those who shed new light on familiar passages,
Who shine new light on to old puzzles:
The joy of the Lord is our strength.
We thank you, for giving us understanding,
For communication by paper and parchment, computer and cartoon:
The joy of the Lord is our strength.

(69) Prayer of Dedication

God, you unite us. We pledge ourselves afresh to work towards
    unity,
To work together to bring justice to the helpless ones,
Healing to the broken ones, refreshment to the weary ones,
To celebrate the unique gifts you have lavished on each one of us.
In the name of Jesus, who died to make us one and set us free.

(70) Prayer of Dismissal

Go to bring good news to the poor, to proclaim release to all who are imprisoned, recovery of sight to the blind, and let the oppressed go free, in the Name of Father, Son and Holy Spirit.

SUNDAY BETWEEN 28 JANUARY AND 3 FEBRUARY

(Fourth Sunday in Ordinary Time)

Jeremiah 1.4–10; Psalm 71.1–6; I Corinthians 13.1–13;
Luke 4.21–30

FULLY KNOWN, FULLY LOVED

Presentation

Illustration: A convex or concave mirror. How does the mirror distort images? Reverses, shrinks, changes dimensions. Show parts of a picture, encouraging guesses about the whole. We only get partial glimpses of God's love now, and our understanding isn't full. We can get things wrong, like misjudging distances in a driving mirror. God has the full picture, to be revealed in the fullness of time.

(71) Call to Worship

Psalm 71.5–6

(72) Prayer of Adoration

Creator God, before our birth, you were planning and perfecting;
In the womb, your care enfolded us with fingers of delicate wonder.
Before our body clocks began to tick, we were destined for love,
And your delivering hand was on your creation.
We awake to adore you.

Comforter God, when our future was still shrouded in darkness,
Your purposes flickered across our hidden future,
Licking the darkness into flames of potential.
You are the one who takes the hand of the child in us,
And tells us: 'Do not be afraid.'
We awake to adore you.

(73) Prayer of Confession

Our strong rock, our castle, we have come to confess our weakness.
Our crag and our stronghold, we have come to confess our fears.
Lord, you took Jeremiah when he thought he was too young to be
   your voice.

So often we use our words wrongly, in cowardly silence, or selfish
  words that damage:
Touch our lips and heal us with your mercy.
You are our hope, O Lord God,
Our confidence since we were young.
When we hang back, feeling too little, too awkward, too
  insignificant:
When we forget your call to be your voice in the world:
Touch our lips and heal us with your mercy.

(74) Prayer of Thanksgiving

Thank you for optimism that triumphs over doubts and difficulties;
Thank you for trusting that triumphs over obstacles and setbacks.
Thank you for empowering the weak, the sidelined, the imperfect:
Thank you, Lord, and praise your Holy Name.

Thank you for vision that sees possibilities in hopeless places;
Thank you for love that sees potential in unexpected people;
Thank you for giving us Jesus, who lived out love in action,
Who walked through a crowd of doubters to set us free:
Thank you, Lord, and praise your Holy Name.

(75) Prayer of Petition

There is a love that is patient, kind and never boastful,
A love that is never irritable or resentful:
**Loving God, may we reflect your love in the mirror of our
  hearts.**

There is a love that never ends, that goes on through all created time,
A love that bears and believes all things, that goes on hoping and
  enduring:
**Loving God, may we reflect your love in the mirror of our
  hearts.**

(76) Prayer of dismissal

I Corinthians 13.12–13

Go in faith, go in hope, go in love,
In the confidence and joy that one day you will fully know, as you
  are fully known,
By your Lord of Love.

SUNDAY BETWEEN 4 AND 10 FEBRUARY

(Fifth Sunday in Ordinary Time)

Isaiah 6.1–8 (9–13); Psalm 138; I Corinthians 15.1–11; Luke 5.1–11

SEND ME!

Presentation
*Illustration: A letter. What do we need to send a letter? An address
– to know where it is going. God has a plan for where he wants
Isaiah, and us, to be. A stamp – to pay for delivery. Sometimes it is
costly and painful to answer God's call. (Isaiah felt unworthy, as did
Jeremiah in last week's lectionary.) A message inside – God gives us
a message of good news to deliver to the world. Jesus is the best
'letter' the world has ever received! We need to respond to God's
call (like the walk to the post-box or letter-box!).*

(77) Call to Worship
Psalm 138.1–3 or the following:

Lord of the lakeside and the lonely way,
Call us into the dance of discipleship here today!
Lord of laden nets and boats and crowded shorelines,
Come into the prow of your church and sail us into worship!

(78) Prayer of Adoration

Life-giver, we come to sing your praise with our whole hearts.
Faith-kindler, we come to glorify your name before all people.
Risk-runner, we come to take risks with you and for you.
Dream-inspirer, we come to shout when you call us, 'Here I am!'
Almighty Creator, we adore you!

(79) Prayer of Confession

Healing God,
Take the live coal from your altar and burn away our uncleanness:
– when we go through the motions of worship without letting your Spirit set us on fire.
– when we look straight through your people who reach out to us in need.
– when we hoard up the gifts you give us and refuse to be used for you.
– when we hurt one another and are too stubborn to put things right.

Healing God,
Take the live coal from your altar and burn away our uncleanness:
– when we are too lazy to go the extra mile for our brothers and sisters.
– when we look no further than our own doorstep and ignore the needs in our world.
– when we waste time talking to put off a moment of action.
– when we long for what is not ours, and forget to celebrate all you have given us.

Healing God,
Take the live coal from your altar and burn away our uncleanness.

(80) Prayer of Thanksgiving

Thank you for your call that came to Simon Peter. You loaded the net with fish, so many it was beginning to break. Thank you, Lord, that Simon knew he was not worthy, but opened himself to be used by you. Thank you for your call to Isaiah; again you used him, cleansing his sin and sending him out when he said 'Here I am!' Thank you, Lord, for your call to Paul, your apostle who knew he was least and lowest, yet you turned his life around and gave him power out of weakness. **Thank you for your call to us; though we too are unworthy, we are here for you!**

(81) Prayer of Dedication

Take who we are, however worthless we feel.
Take what we have, however small and silly it may seem.
Take what we can be and help us each day to move towards that
goal in you.

(82) Prayer of Dismissal

Go from this place of prayer, that is God's temple,
Back into the place of prayer that is God's world.
Go, rejoicing in his calling, celebrating his Kingdom and walking
    in his grace.

SUNDAY BETWEEN 11 AND 17 FEBRUARY

(Sixth Sunday in Ordinary Time)

Jeremiah 17.5–10; Psalm 1; I Corinthians 15.12–20; Luke 6.17–26

ROOTS BY THE STREAM

Presentation
Illustration: A pot plant. Most plants need water to survive. Where does the plant get its water? Where do we get our spiritual 'water' from? How do we make sure our roots remain in God? Leaves, fruits etc. cannot form healthily without roots and water. Neither can we be the best we can be if we aren't 'planted by the stream' of God's love. Contrast what Jeremiah says about trusting only in people, which leads to 'parched places' in the desert. What are the effects in our lives without God?

(83) Call to Worship

Jeremiah 17.7–8 or Psalm 1.1–3

(84) Prayer of Adoration

Gardener God, you made the rushing rivers and the oceans that lap our planet;
You refresh thirsty roots with rain and bring out good fruit in season.
Plant us by the water, and send out our roots by the stream.
Gardener God, you tenderly irrigate desert places, blessing your world
With cool winds and soft breezes; in you, when the heat comes, leaves stay green.
Plant us by the water, and send out our roots by the stream.
Gardener God, you have given resources to bring relief to those who are in barren places,
Trusting us to drink from you and to share your fruits with the hungry.
Plant us by the water, and send out our roots by the stream.

(85) Prayer of Confession

Refresh us with the streams of your mercy.
When we wander from your way, pulling up our roots or planting
  them in the shallow sand;
When we sunbathe in sin and selfishness and our mouths grow
  parched without your word:
Refresh us with the streams of your mercy.
When we trust in human wisdom and worldly solutions,
When we feel over-confident in our own wisdom and judgments:
Refresh us with the streams of your mercy.

(86) Prayer of Thanksgiving

Blessed are the poor:
Thank you, God of all, for the promise of your Kingdom.
Blessed are those who hunger now:
Thank you, God of all, for the promise to satisfy.
Blessed are those who weep now:
Thank you, God of all, for the foretaste of laughter.
Blessed are the excluded and insulted:
Thank you, God of all, for Heaven's reward foreshadowed.

(87) Meditation

Watering the garden in the soft light of evening,
The hosepipe's steady stream suddenly faltered.
I looked round, indignantly, for the one who had stood on the green
  coils in the grass.
Nobody was there. Then I saw that the nozzle lay detached from
  the tap.
I feel so weary today, Lord. It's so long since I sat at your feet.
I listen to so many voices, cynical, boasting, full of hard-headed
  advice.
I'm aching and empty and broken, and beached here like a fish out
  of water.
Just reaching out to you, I let myself feel your refreshment,
Soothing my deepest roots with cooling water of life,
Flushing out all my failures, and welling up like unwept tears of joy.

(88) Prayer of Dismissal

Go, like trees planted by streams of water, to bear fruit in due season,
with leaves that do not wither, rooted and grounded in God.

SUNDAY BETWEEN 18 AND 24 FEBRUARY

(Seventh Sunday in Ordinary Time)

Genesis 45.3–11, 15; Psalm 37.1–11, 39–40;
I Corinthians 15.35–38, 42–50; Luke 6.27–38

FORGIVING AND FORGIVEN

Presentation

Illustration: Act out a petty quarrel, about stolen sweets or an insult, for example. Act it twice, with alternative endings of forgiving/ unforgiving reactions. It would be useful to 'freeze-frame' the action in order to get the congregation thinking about how they might react, what they might say next. How do we heal rifts? Wounds only heal when they get air. It's no use simply sticking a plaster on forever. Joseph had to move in forgiveness to his brothers. Forgiveness is costly, but worthwhile if we are to move forward. Jesus reminds us to 'do-as-we-would-be-done-by' in this.

(89) Call to Worship

Psalm 37.5–6 or the following:

Let us take delight in the Lord, for he will give us our heart's desire:
Let us commit our way to the Lord, and put our trust in him.

(90) Prayer of Adoration

Glorious God, we come before you, to worship and adore.
You have brought us from warm, comfortable beds,
The fantastic smell of bacon and the crunch of breakfast cereals.
You have brought us with friends and companions to the door of
 your house;
You have welcomed us in to gather as your family:
Glorious God, we come before you, to worship and adore.

All the world is yours, the pleasures of home, and the beauty of
 creation,
The impulse deep within us to seek your face.
Together we praise you for such a privilege,
To learn about you, pray to you, sing to you, share our lives with you,

The Creator of the world, the God of abundant life:
Glorious God, we come before you, to worship and adore.

(91) Prayer of Confession

When we are cold and unforgiving, bearing grudges and nursing
old wounds:
Mercy incarnate, forgive.
When we plan revenge in little spiteful ways and think nobody sees:
Mercy incarnate, forgive.
When we keep our distance and make enemies of friends:
Mercy incarnate, forgive.
Joseph said to his brothers: 'Come closer to me.' And they came
closer.
When we refuse to do the same:
Mercy incarnate, forgive.
Jesus said: 'Forgive, and you will be forgiven.' Take all the
unforgiveness stored in our hearts.
Silence
Mercy incarnate, forgive.

(92) Prayer of Petition

God of all glory, break down the barriers, melt our unforgiving
hearts,
Give us the compassion that turns around gently instead of turning
our backs,
Give us your love in place of our indifference, and bring us to your
peace.

(93) Prayer of Dismissal

Go in the promise that what was sown in weakness will be raised in
power.
Go in the hope that what is sown in dishonour will be raised in glory.
Go in the pardon of the just judge, who calls you into his presence,
To forgive as you are forgiven.
We go rejoicing, restored and ready!

SUNDAY BETWEEN 25 AND 29 FEBRUARY

(Eighth Sunday in Ordinary Time)

Ecclesiasticus 27.4–7 or Isaiah 55.10–13; Psalm 92.1–4, 12–15;
I Corinthians 15.51–58; Luke 6.39–49

BUILDING ON THE ROCK

Presentation
Illustration: Two teams try to build a structure with building bricks, one on a firm table, the other on a cushion or similar unsteady surface. Or build a house of cards and get someone to blow on it! Building is a tricky business. We need to choose the right materials, and the right location. Draw out: What building bricks does Jesus give us? His teachings, his commandments, his example of love, etc. We have to use them to make our faith secure.

(94) Call to Worship

Psalm 92.1–4

(95) Prayer of Adoration

Nurturing, nourishing God, you have made all things through your
    Word,
Shaping and moulding with an imagination that leaps through
    starry spaces, stirs the elements in a cosmic soup of surprises,
    bringing order out of chaos and rhythm out of discord.
It is a good thing to give thanks to the Lord:
And to sing praises to your name, O most high!
God, you craft and care for the broad sweep of the universe and the
    intimate detail on the feather of the sparrow and the expressions
    on our faces.
Even the mountains and the hills burst into song to know you are
    the Creator,
Even the trees clap their hands to worship their Lord.
It is a good thing to give thanks to the Lord:
And to sing praises to your name, O most high!

(96) Prayer of Thanksgiving

Read I Corinthians 15.51–58

God, we have listened to your mystery, your amazing plan for the
  fullness of time.
We do not ask to know what you mean by the last trumpet,
Or how long is the twinkling of an eye.
We only thank you for the promise of eternal life, imperishable,
  immortal,
And that it is through Jesus Christ our Lord that such a future is for
  those who love him.
We thank you that death has been defused by the light of your
  victory.
We thank you that death has been disarmed of its sting, as Jesus
  takes our sins upon him.
We thank you for the Holy Spirit who draws us into communion
  with you,
And we receive your promise that the labours of building your
  Kingdom here on earth
Will not be in vain.

(97) Prayer of Confession

Gentle God, sometimes things can get in the way of seeing you:
They get in the way of seeing our neighbour's point of view,
They get in the way of our doing your will.
Take away our sin and make us whole.
Patient God, forgive us for the times we have led people astray,
So confident we are walking in the right direction.
Take away our sin and make us whole.
Trustworthy God, you know we sometimes build on shaky
  foundations,
Trying to bodge and take shortcuts and cut all the corners;
We want to get there yesterday, and meet ourselves coming back.
Take away our sin and make us whole.
Supportive God, you are the rock we want to build on,
So that no cold winds can blow away what we build in your name.
Take away our sin and make us whole.

(98) Prayer of Dedication

Take us, in our stumbling walk and plant our feet on the rock.
Take us, full of contradictions and imperfections and make
   something beautiful for your delight.
Take all we have to offer and use us powerfully, that your word
   may return to you fulfilled in love.

(99) Prayer of Dismissal

The Lord will lead us out rejoicing, and lead us home again in his
peace.

SUNDAY BEFORE LENT

Exodus 34.29–35; Psalm 99; II Corinthians 3.12–4.2;
Luke 9.28–36 (37–43)

WITH UNVEILED FACES

Presentation
*Illustration: Play 'Kim's Game' where objects hidden by a cloth are
briefly revealed before being covered again while the congregation
attempts to remember as many objects as possible. What was it like
when the cloth was put back on? We are eager to take it off again to
see if we had remembered rightly! Display some objects that protect
(some of these might be suitable for inclusion in the game above);
talk about why we need oven gloves, welding masks, cycle helmets,
goggles, sunblock? Why did Moses need the veil? The sight of God
would be much more overwhelming than fire or even the sun! Jesus
displayed God's glory, but he made it possible for us to come face to
face with God, faces unveiled.*

(100) Call to Worship

Psalm 99.1–3 or 4–5

(101) Prayer of Adoration

God of glory, we come before you to confess your name which is
  great and awesome.
The Lord our God is the Holy One.
You are the lover of justice, you come to establish righteousness on
  earth as in Heaven.
The Lord our God is the Holy One.
In the time of Moses, the people called to you, and you answered
  them, you spoke to them out of the pillar of cloud.
The Lord our God is the Holy One.
Proclaim the greatness of the Lord our God, and let us worship him
  on his holy hill.
The Lord our God is the Holy One.

(102) Meditation

Read Luke 9.28–36

Here on the mountainside I try to remember.
Did it really happen here? I thought I was dreaming, my eyes heavy
with sleep.
We had struggled to stay awake, John and James and I,
Always afraid to miss the extraordinary that Jesus could mint out of
ordinary things.
Suddenly that light, brighter than sun and casting no shadow,
Filling our Jesus, his familiar face and shape, with a gifting glow
like all the angels of Heaven.
The words escape, the images remain. Burning like the bush, but
not consumed,
Radiant, incandescent, but who were his companions?
I thought I knew and I stammered when it was almost over:
'Master, it is good for us to be here; let us make some tents for
you, and Moses and Elijah!'
What was I saying? But such compassion in his face as the glow was
fading,
He understood my confusion, held my terror like a question mark for
later.
Then that cloud and a voice that spoke like lightning, thundering its
arc from pole to pole;
'This is my Son, my Chosen; listen to him!'
My bursting eardrums and frightened eyes he held in his humble
gaze,
As if unveiling the face of God.
We stood in the silence, changed in a world that was forever
changed.

(103) Prayer of Thanksgiving

Transfiguring, transforming Saviour, tearing the veil that hides and
bringing us close,
We thank you for the hope we have, that we may move forward
boldly,
Overshadowed by the cloud, and sure of the voice that calls.
Thank you for the Spirit, who brings us freedom,
For the privilege of walking in your light with our faces turned
unveiled to you.

(104) Prayer of Dedication

We cast aside the things that bind us, our narrow vision, peeping
    through our fingers;
Polish us as mirrors you have made to reflect your glory, and
    transform us in your image,
As we were born to be. What we have seen, may we never forget;
Keep the vision of your loveliness imprinted on our lives,
That by the Holy Spirit we too may show your glory
To those still waiting at the foot of the mountain.

(105) Prayer of Dismissal

Go now, to be God's witnesses in the world, reflecting in the mirror
of faith the glory of the Father, the obedience of the Son and the
overspreading power of the Holy Spirit.

ASH WEDNESDAY

Joel 2.1–2, 12–17 or Isaiah 58.1–12; Psalm 51.1–17;
II Corinthians 5.20b–6.10; Matthew 6.1–6, 16–21

YOUR TREASURE AND YOUR HEART

Presentation

*Illustration: Hide a 'treasure' (a coin, ring or watch will suffice)
borrowed from a member of the congregation under one of three
upturned cups at the front of the church. Invite them to follow its
progress as you shuffle the cups around. Were they right? Draw out
how they followed their token treasure with their eyes, their head,
their concentration, so as not to lose track of it. Would we be willing
to offer something precious if we risked losing it? Ask what people
have chosen to give up for Lent. Jesus taught us that we should place
our most treasured things in God's hands, with all our heart. Share
a time of quietness, with the opportunity to reconsider what we might
offer to God this Lent.*

(106) Call to Worship

Create a clean heart in me, O God:
And renew a right spirit within me.

(107) Prayer of Adoration and Dedication

God of this Lenten season, you prepare our hearts for the coming
   sacrifice.
You are the one who changed the world with your costly gift on the
   cruel cross:
God, whom we adore, we come before you to be changed.
You healed our darkness with the flood of Easter light;
Blossoming out of the barren landscape of Lent:
God, whom we adore, we come before you to be healed.
We worship you as the one who is worthy of all adoration,
Who alone can prepare us for the coming days:
God, whom we adore, we come before you to be prepared.
Giver of all, our Guide and Provider,
Let our fast be acceptable as we proclaim your glory:
**God, whom we adore, we come before you to give you all
   honour and praise.**

(108) Prayer of confession

When we hold back the best and offer you second best:
Forgive us, in your mercy.
When we dwell on our sins and lose heart to ask forgiveness:
Forgive us, in your mercy.
When we make a huge show of what we have given up for you:
Forgive us, in your mercy.
When we give so everyone knows what we have given:
Forgive us, in your mercy.

(109) Prayer of Petition

Give us the humility to walk the way ahead with integrity;
Teach us to loosen the bonds laid on your people, through debts
    and false expectations, through poverty, crime and rejection;
May our fast be the one you have chosen, to bring the homeless to
    our table, to clothe the humiliated with tenderness, and to be
    patient with those who are closest to us.

(110) Prayer of Thanksgiving

**O God, who sees in secret, we thank you for secret rewards to
    treasure.**
In a season of penitence, we thank you for all we will be learning.
In a season of reflection, we thank you for your presence with us in
    quiet places.
In a season of sacrifice, we thank you for the joy to which you call
    us,
As we go thankfully, with shining faces, walking with our God.
**O God, who sees in secret, we thank you for secret rewards to
    treasure.**

(111) Prayer of Dismissal

Now may the Lord who loves you more than you can imagine, keep
you in times of temptation, delight you in times of discovery, and
hold you in times of struggle, until you see his face.

FIRST SUNDAY IN LENT

Deuteronomy 26.1–11; Psalm 91.1–2, 9–16; Romans 10.8b–13; `
Luke 4.1–13

THE WORD IS NEAR YOU

Presentation

Illustration: Tray of cakes or box of chocolates. Ask who has given up sweet things for Lent. Ask them what they feel when they see the 'temptation' on the tray. Who would they be letting down if they gave in? God? Themselves? Family? Discuss if some things are more tempting than others (i.e. the smell of baking bread, the chance to lie in when you should be somewhere else). Read the three temptations the devil set before Jesus. Which seems most tempting? Immediate gratification, power, worshipping the wrong thing (what might such things be in our lives?), and putting God to the test are all involved. List similar temptations in our modern world, and pray for Jesus' strength in resisting.

(112) Call to Worship

Let us worship the Lord in times of trouble.
You are our refuge and our stronghold, our God in whom we put our trust.
Let us worship the Lord in moments of temptation.
You are our refuge and our stronghold, our God in whom we put our trust.
Let us worship the Lord in the trials and triumphs of life.
You are our refuge and our stronghold, our God in whom we put our trust.

(113) Meditation

Silence, possibly with soothing music
Temptations tease us and snatch away our peace. Voices pull us this way and that.
Sights make us open our eyes wide, sweet smells set our nostrils twitching.
Our muscles tense with resisting and restlessness, summoning up the strength to say 'no'.
Suddenly, another voice comes over the waves of whispers and dares.

This voice is gentleness, knowing our struggles:
'The word is near you; on your lips and in your heart.'
The murmurings of temptation recede. We relax into the truth.
God is not far away, tutting and testing. He is closer than a heartbeat,
Arming us with his strength.

(114) Prayer of Adoration

Energetic Creator, delivering and protecting your people, you spread
   your shelter over us wherever we walk. Your name is love:
And we adore you.
Understanding Christ, you have walked every step before us,
   resisting the darkness, faithful to the Father. Your name is love:
And we adore you.
Powerful Spirit, you drive us and direct us, pushing us and
   challenging us, and breathing in your healing strength. Your
   name is love:
And we adore you.

(115) Prayer of Confession

God, in your Word, you tell us that those who call on your name,
   you will answer.
We call on your name, confessing our weakness and wilfulness.
We call on your name, confessing our shallowness, our commitment
   like butterflies in the wind.
We call on your name, confessing our shadowy, flickering love,
And as we call on your name, we listen for your word of grace and
   healing.
Silence
Your answer never fails us: 'Rise, refreshed, for your sins are
   washed whiter than snow.'
Like the flowers pushing their way into Spring, we open ourselves
   to your sunshine and shalom.

(116) Prayer of Thanksgiving

Thank you, Creator, for the days when trials come, for they come
   with opportunities.
Thank you, Jesus, for the times you come to us, struggling at our
   side.
Thank you, Holy Spirit, for the times when Lent clears away the
   clutter and we hear you sing.

(117) Prayer of Dedication

Take our resolve, and strengthen it.
Take our determination, and bolster it.
Take our weakness, and transform it.
Take our gifts, graces, time and talents, and make them ever your
  own.

(118) Prayer of Dismissal

Fill us with your strength to keep us moving, fill us with your
gentleness to come alongside our brothers and sisters, fill us with
your love to bring us through all we may meet in the knowledge that
we are yours.

SECOND SUNDAY IN LENT

Genesis 15.1–12, 17–18; Psalm 27; Philippians 3.17–4.1; Luke 13.31–35

THE HEN AND HER CHICKS

Presentation

Illustration: Video clip or pictures of birds, animals and humans protecting their young. Talk about the images. What things do parents worry about on behalf of their children? Is there a point when the young want to strike out on their own? Ask mothers when they stop being mothers (never!). God in Jesus never stops caring. Do we find the image of the mother hen startling? Even in danger and disobedience, Jesus longs to gather us together.

(119) Call to Worship

Psalm 27.1 or 4

(120) Prayer of Adoration

God, you are everything to your children.
Loving and nurturing like a mother or a father, fierce to protect us,
Always wanting the very best for us.
Like all that is best in mothers and fathers, you follow us with your eye,
Tender when we stumble, firm when we stray.
Fatherly, motherly God, we adore you for such a love.

God, you are everything to your people.
We long to come into your house, and to live where you are,
In your church and in the world.
Precious, parenting God, we cannot turn from the love that circles us,
You are singing away our secret fears, and wiping away our hidden tears.
Fatherly, motherly God, we adore you for such a love.

Your love holds us together as a family, even when we struggle to go our own way,
When we run and hide and do our own thing.
You are the Carer, the Nurturer, the Friend, who weans us, watches us learn to walk,

And goes on loving your wayward ones.
Fatherly, motherly God, we adore you for such a love.

(121) Prayer of Confession

Lord we confess to you, and call on you to save us from ourselves.
The Lord is my light
And my salvation.
Save us from ourselves when we alienate ourselves from those who
    long to love us.
When we are arrogant, wilful and disobedient in the light of your
    love.
The Lord is my light
And my salvation.
Save us from ourselves when we set our minds on earthly things,
When we forget to act justly, like citizens of Heaven.
The Lord is my light
And my salvation.

Save us from ourselves when we fail to stand firm in your love,
When we deny your lordship in our lives, strutting and preening as
    if we did not know Jesus.
The Lord is my light
And my salvation.

(122) Prayer of Thanksgiving

You promised Abraham you were his shield, you gave him a vision
    of land for his children.
We thank you for promises that are easy to believe, and those that
    increase our sense of wonder.
You gave to Paul a joy and concern for your people.
We thank you for gifts that fill us with rejoicing, and those that
    challenge us to act for others.
You speak in our hearts: 'Seek my face,' and we long to know you
    more and more.
We thank you for your closeness to us, and the mystery that keeps
    us exploring your greatness.

(123) Prayer of Dedication

As you have been a Father to us,
Make us more loving to our sisters and brothers.
As you have been a Mother to us,
Make us more loving to our sisters and brothers.
As you have loved us with a love that will not give us up,
Make us more loving to our sisters and brothers.

(124) Prayer of Dismissal

Psalm 27.13–14 read responsively

THIRD SUNDAY IN LENT

Isaiah 55.1–9; Psalm 63.1–8; I Corinthians 10.1–13; Luke 13.1–9

COME TO THE WATERS

Presentation

Illustration: Divide the congregation in half; give one side small candles and let them spread the flame from wick to wick from a taper at the front until all the candles are alight. At the same time, pass a tube of sweets around the other half. Ask who still has something left after a few moments? The sweets may well have looked tempting, but they did not last at all. There may not have been enough for everyone. The candles, like the provision of God, go on burning long afterwards. The choices we make are not always wise ones. God's ways and thoughts, says Isaiah, are not ours. We can trust his free invitation to the waters of life.

(125) Call to Worship

Isaiah 55.1–2 or Psalm 63.1–4 read by different voices

(126) Prayer of Adoration

God of the moment and God of eternity,
We come before you, thirsty for the waters that last and satisfy:
God, we love you, and eagerly we seek you.
God of great changes and God who is changeless,
We come before you, singing your praises and seeking your will:
God, we love you, and eagerly we seek you.
God of grace and God of glory,
We come before you, glad that you are our Maker, telling out your
    matchless majesty:
God, we love you, and eagerly we seek you.

(127) Prayer of Confession

Read I Corinthians 10.1–13

Patient Friend, like the children of Israel, we eat and drink and play without a thought for you. Like them, we go astray, and put Christ to the test. We grumble and complain, seeing situations, people and problems from our narrow angle. Paul warned us that when we think we are standing safe, we should be watchful that we do not fall. We often think we are safe, dependent on nobody. We manage our money without caring for those who have less. We live as we choose to, without listening to those who know better. You will never test us beyond our strength. As we become conscious of the wrongs we have done so freely, we lay these burdens at your feet, humbly asking for you to forgive us.

Silence

Your right hand holds us fast, God of all Mercy. You lift us from our knees to freedom and a new start as fresh as the water that flows from your grace. We are forgiven. We are at one with you once more.

(128) Prayer of Thanksgiving

For love without limit, and water flowing free,
For wine, milk and bread without money or price to satisfy,
For sins forgiven and broken hearts bound up,
For second chances, to bear fruit where we once seemed barren:
We give you thanks and praise.

(129) Prayer of Petition

Where we are satisfied with what cannot last, change our appetite
for your living food.
Where we are satisfied to maintain the status quo, lead us to
adventure that extra mile.
Where we are satisfied to trust our own ideas, make us more
curious to discover yours.
Where we are satisfied with less than abundant life, make our thirst
more acute to taste your fullness.

(130) Prayer of Dedication

Take our gifts, Loving God, for they come from your bounty.
Take our imperfect lives and pour in the reality and colour of your
perfection.
Take all our trying and trifling, and let the spirit of Love sweep in
to transform all we attempt in your name.

(131) Prayer of Dismissal

Refreshed by the water that quenches our deepest thirst,
empowered by the Spirit of Christ that calls us and keeps us,
blessed by the love of God, who is faithful for ever and ever:
We go, to live and work to God's glory.

FOURTH SUNDAY IN LENT

(Mothering Sunday)

Joshua 5.9–12 (Exodus 2.1–10; I Samuel 1.20–28); Psalm 32
(Psalms 34.11–20; 127.1–4); II Corinthians 5.16–21
(II Corinthians 1.3–7; Colossians 3.12–17); Luke 15. 1–3, 11b-32
(Luke 2.33–35; John 19.25–27)

COMING HOME

Presentation

*Illustration: Large board game, dice and two teams racing to get
'home' (numbered squares of paper laid like two paths on the floor
leading to two hoops. Play like Ludo.) When one team has won, draw
out what it felt like to get near home. Anticipation, relief, joy may be
experienced. Are we glad to get home from a holiday? Talk about
coming home to God, reconciled through Christ (I Corinthians
5.16–21) and the wayward son in Luke. Now return to the teams and
tell them there is a prize for the winner. Give it to the loser instead.
Is that fair? Explore the feelings of the brother who thought he had
done everything right, but did not get the party and the fatted calf.*

(132) Call to Worship

Psalm 32.11 or the following:

Come all who are in Christ:
In Christ there is a new creation.
Everything old has passed away:
See, everything has become new!
All this is from God:
Who reconciled us to himself through Christ.
Let us worship the Lord and join his ministry of reconciliation.

(133) Prayer of Adoration

God, our hiding-place, our homecoming,
You surround us with shouts of deliverance.
Shout for joy, all you who are true of heart:
Be glad, you righteous and rejoice in the Lord!

You are like a beacon in the darkness,
A lighthouse in a sea boiling and raging,
A place where we can find our bearings and plan new journeys.
Shout for joy, all you who are true of heart:
Be glad, you righteous and rejoice in the Lord!

Lord, you bring home the wanderer, and party with those who repent,
You love knows no limits or boundaries,
We rejoice that when we stray, we see you from far off,
Running to greet us with robes of rejoicing.
Shout for joy, all you who are true of heart:
Be glad, you righteous and rejoice in the Lord!

(134) Prayer of Confession

In times of trouble, we come to you, faithful God,
To acknowledge our guilt and confess our sin.
The psalmist has sung of your forgiveness.
We want to be counted in the number of those who are happy,
Because you have taken their sins away.
We will not conceal our guilt, Lord. In the silence we tell you
    where we have gone wrong.
Silence
Blessed by your mercy, lifted by your healing, we receive your
    pardon and rejoice.

(135) Prayer of Thanksgiving

*If possible, with a roving microphone, gather a list of reasons to
rejoice from the congregation. After each join in the following
thanksgiving:*

God, you fill our lives with reasons to rejoice.
Our hearts overflow with thanks to the King.

(136) Prayer of Petition

God of Love, you welcome us all into the family of Christ;
But on this Mothering Sunday, we have all travelled from different
    places;
Some of us are nuclear families, parents with children,
Some of us are single, and glad of it, or sad with it!
Some of us miss partners, who used to sit beside us,
Some of us are separated, working through painful emotions.

Others of us don't know where we fit into the neat time-honoured
    patterns.
Give us the grace to be sensitive with one another, making no
    assumptions,
Except that we all belong.

(137) Prayer of Dedication

Take our laughter, our loving, our complicated relationships,
Take our broken hearts and our contentment, our meetings and
    partings.
You accept us as we are; we pledge ourselves to accept each other
    for your sake.

(138) Prayer of Dismissal

Wherever you go from here, whoever you meet on your way,
    whatever your hopes and dreams,
Go with the God who loves you and welcomes you home to his
    heart.

FIFTH SUNDAY IN LENT

(First Sunday of the Passion)

Isaiah 43.16–21; Psalm 126; Phillippians 3.4b-14; John 12.1–8

AN EXTRAVAGANT GIFT

Presentation

Illustration: A present. This could belong to the preacher or a member of the congregation and should have been given for no special reason (an 'un-birthday' gift!).When we love someone very much, we often express it in extravagant ways. Mary's costly perfume seemed scandalous to Judas, who had his own hidden agenda. God's love goes beyond our deserving. Read Psalm 126. The laughter and shouts of joy show us how overwhelming God's love can be. How do we express our love in return?

(139) Call to Worship

God has invited us in with extravagant love.
We come in with joy and shouts of laughter!
God has invited us in to meet with him today.
We come to meet our Lord with songs of joy!

(140) Prayer of Adoration

Enduring God, as we come to worship you on Passion Sunday,
We recognize the joy that lies beyond the deep agony.
You are the God of Love, not tight-lipped and grudging love,
But love that laid down its life through Jesus,
To take us through the darkest gulf of fear and pain to meet with
   Paradise.
Who has done all this?
Our God whom we adore, who died that we might live.

Suffering God, as we trace your journey to the cross,
And see betrayal and pain in your eyes,
We marvel at your love that looked beyond the grave.
You made the world, and set the boundaries of sea and land,
You formed us from the first to know you as our everything.
Yet still you shrunk yourself to meet the wrench of death for us.
Who has done all this?
Our God whom we adore, who died that we might live.

(141) Prayer of Petition

Read Philippians 3.4b-14

God of all grace and power,
Like Paul we know we have not yet reached our goal.
As we press on towards the greatest prize,
The heavenly call of God in Jesus Christ,
We only ask this, humbly, seeking your help:
May we not be afraid to suffer for your sake,
May we never shrink from standing at your side.
May we choose your precious love above all the gains this world
can offer.

(142) Prayer of Thanksgiving

For dreams of sunshine through the storm-clouds:
We thank you, suffering Saviour.
For the promise of deliverance beyond despair:
We thank you, suffering Saviour.
For the glimpse of new joy beyond present weeping:
We thank you, suffering Saviour.
For the hope of Heaven after this life on earth:
We thank you, suffering Saviour.

(143) Prayer of Dedication

Mary smashed a pot of precious nard, flooding the house with its
perfume.
She opened her hands to risky giving and let down her hair to wipe.
Now we open our hands and let down our hair for you.
Accept our offering of love, for we want to give not meanly,
looking over our shoulders, but gladly, colourfully, because your
love overwhelms our hearts.

(144) Prayer of Dismissal

As you have gathered us, Spirit of Passion,
Now send us on our way, your way, to fill the world with the
perfume of your presence,
And tell out the wonder of the extravagant love of God.

SIXTH SUNDAY IN LENT

(Second Sunday of the Passion/Palm Sunday)

Isaiah 50.4–9a; Psalm 118.1–2,19–29 (or Psalm 31.9–16);
Philippians 2.5–11; Matthew 21.1–11 (Luke 23.1–49)

SHOUTING STONES

Presentation
*Illustration: A jacket or coat. Lay this down, if possible at the Palm
Procession if this takes place at the beginning of the service. Why
were the cloaks laid down? Talk about red carpets laid for important
guests and the legend of Raleigh's cloak, the puddle and Elizabeth
the First. We want to express our worship for Jesus by showing he is
important. To lay down cloaks or palm leaves we have to bob down
and bow! Jesus said even the stones would shout! Make a list of
things in creation which worship in their own way, according to the
Bible (sun, moon, trees, mountains etc.)*

(145) Call to Worship

*Psalm 118.1, 19 and 21; Psalm 31.14–16, or Luke 19.38, which
could be shouted together*

(146) Prayer of Adoration

There is a buzz in the air today, and the streets are filled with
    shouting.
This is the Lord's doing! Nothing can stop the journey now
    beginning:
Blessed is the King who comes in the name of the Lord!
Peace in heaven and glory in the highest!
On a saddle of cloaks, riding on a colt, the King is coming to his
    people.
Running the gauntlet of cheering and secret mockery,
Blessed is the King who comes in the name of the Lord!
Peace in heaven and glory in the highest!
Let us celebrate with waving palms and dancing hearts,
Even the stones would shout if we were silent!
Blessed is the King who comes in the name of the Lord!
Peace in heaven and glory in the highest!

(147) Meditation or Prayer of Confession

Jesus, as you pass by in the noisy procession, we close our eyes. Jostled this way and that by swaying bodies, we find ourselves pushed to the back of the crowd. The sounds of shouting grow fainter. Now we can hear ourselves think, and the thoughts that come clamouring shame us. Will we follow you all the way, or enjoy the holiday atmosphere, singing and dancing, then scuttle away home to comfort and peace? We confess we are afraid where all this fuss will lead you. The doubters and plotters are gathering for the kill. We listen to their sniping and nod, saying nothing in your defence, even though we know you and profess we love you. We are not worthy that you should even look at us as you ride on the way love must take you. But we push our way back to the front of the crush and cry out for your forgiveness:

Hosanna, Lord, hosanna! **Hosanna, Lord, hosanna!**
Hosanna, Lord, now save us! **Hosanna, Lord, now save us!**
Your mercy endures forever. Healed and forgiven we follow you
on your way.

(148) Prayer of Thanksgiving

Jesus, as we walk with you on Palm Sunday, thank you that you
did not stay in heaven,
Leaving us to go our own way.
Thank you for the humility that brought you to earth to live our
human life,
Walking on the stony road that led to terror and abandonment.
Thank you that you emptied yourself of all you might have clung
on to,
The power to choose a simpler, less messy end, out of the public
eye.
Thank you for loving us enough to do this, for drawing us into the
most wonderful story
That could happen in any millennium since the creation of the world.

(149) Prayer of Dedication

You are our God: **Our times are in your hand**.
We want to go on singing your praises, when the crowds have
dispersed,
And the sun is hidden behind the cloud.

We want to go on telling your story, when the road gets steeper
And our tired eyes turn to the cross.
You are our God: **Our times are in your hand.**

(150) Prayer of Dismissal

We go forward on the journey, bearing palms of praise as we sing to
the king, bearing signs of hope to keep this joy deep in our hearts,
bearing echoes of 'Hosanna' to bring us by faith to salvation.

HOLY WEEK

Isaiah 50.4–9a; Psalm 70; Hebrews 12.1–3; John 13.21–32

MOCKED AND REJECTED

Presentation

Illustration: Harmless insults played on a tape or written on cards. How do we react? Laughter, embarrassment, feelings of rejection? Compare the kind of insults thrown at Jesus during Holy Week.None of these was said in fun. Often insults are exchanged when people are already feeling low. How does this make us feel? Do we 'give as good as we get' when people tease or insult us. Jesus never did. Contrast the way our reactions or silences can be signs of strength or weakness. Jesus was a new kind of hero. People find it hard to cope with this!

(151) Call to Worship

Psalm 70.1–2 or Isaiah 50.4–7

(152) Prayer of Adoration

Faithful Creator, every morning you wake us to worship,
As the sun breaks free from the horizon,
As the tides ebb and flow on the shores of islands and continents.
Faithful Creator: **We worship you with heart, mind and spirit.**

Faithful Christ, you did not turn away at the hour of betrayal.
When blackest night descended with the shadows of rejection,
You set your face nobly for the final hour.
Faithful Christ: **We worship you with heart, mind and spirit.**

Faithful Spirit, you teach and coax us, bearing with our slowness,
You pray for us and in us, soft as a whisper, gentle as a dove,
Yet constant as fire, warming and thawing our stubborn hearts.
Faithful Spirit: **We worship you with heart, mind and spirit.**

(153) Prayer of Confession

Our God, you were betrayed, insulted by those closest to you.
We need to tell you about our own betrayals,
The insults we have freely heaped on others.
We have betrayed you, preferring our own needs to those of others.

We have betrayed you, talking about your will and not doing it.
We have insulted you, speaking carelessly to fragile people.
We have insulted you, forgetting to live as your children.
For betrayals and insults, forgive us:
Heal us and lead us forward in your name.

(154) Prayer of Thanksgiving

For Jesus' faithfulness when times were unbearably stressful,
For Jesus' courage when the going got tough,
For Jesus' willingness to endure all things for our sake:
Sisters and brothers in Christ, let us thank God together.
For opportunities to stand firm under stresses and rebuffs,
For chances to show courage when things do not go as we expect,
For the road that leads us in the steps of our Saviour:
Sisters and brothers in Christ, let us thank God together.

(155) Prayer of Petition

When the way gets rougher, rockier and steeper under our feet:
Give us your determination to finish the climb.
When the days get darker, under the shadow of the cross:
Give us your determination to embrace God's will.
When the challenges and options get more bewildering:
Give us your determination to choose what is right and follow it.

(156) Prayer of Dedication

Saviour, you do not need shallow promises or easy declarations.
You have been betrayed before.
Only help us to trace your steps with respect and wonder,
Gaining in insight and tolerance for one another,
Learning from your trials and tasting the tears,
Until the day when we know as we are fully known.

(157) Prayer of Dismissal

Trace the path of Christ and plant your feet in his footsteps. Go from this place knowing you are part of the purposes of the Creator, the struggle of Christ and the triumph of the Holy Spirit.

MAUNDY THURSDAY

Exodus 12.1–4 (5–10) 11–14; Psalm 116.1–2,12–19;
I Corinthians 11.23–26; John 13. 1–17

IN REMEMBRANCE OF ME

Presentation
Illustration: Photographs and souvenirs. What memories do these items bring to mind? People, places, feelings. Show the bread and wine. Remind the congregation what Jesus said about doing this in remembrance of him. Are actions even more powerful than flat images and pictures? Do we sometimes do things the way we saw someone close doing them? Draw out: how certain smells, sights, tastes take us right back to a moment in time, or bring a loved one to mind. Memories don't just look backwards. They sustain us in the present, too. We never lose people while we have memories. Jesus comes into our life now through these tokens of his life and death.

(158) Call to Worship
Psalm 116.12–14 or the following:

Lord of Bread, we come to remember and worship you.
Lord of Wine, we come to drink and be satisfied.
Lord of Footwashing, we come to be cleansed by your gesture of love.
We will lift up the cup of salvation,
And call upon the name of the Lord.

(159) Prayer of Adoration

Humble Lord God, who stooped down to take the ordinary, the bread of the field from the golden grain, the wine from the heavy grapes on the vine; we worship you for taking and transforming the everyday food into an extraordinary feast, that echoes down the ages, gathering in your people.
Humble Lord God, we adore you and long to share your feast.

Humble Lord God, who stooped down to wash the feet of your disciples, gently bathing away the traces of the dust, tenderly soothing the aches of long journeying, we worship you for the care that takes the task of a servant and transforms it into the service of a friend.
Humble Lord God, we adore you and offer ourselves to be washed by your love.

(160) Prayer of Confession

Lord, we come with heavy hearts; you said to your disciples:
'Little children, I am with you only a little longer.'
Yet even now, we act as if we had all the time,
All the space, all the leisure in the world to put things right.
We are lulled by our own laziness, putting off saying sorry.
We are too vain to let you wash our feet,
Too proud to bend down to wash the feet of a stranger;
Too busy to give each other time, we bustle through our lives,
Emails and memoranda, and no time to stop and serve.
We are hungry for trivia, food that does not last,
Dizzy with doing, too self-important to calm down the pace.
Forgive us and feed us. Refresh us and give us to drink.
Remake us, kneeling with the towel at our feet.

(161) Meditation

Jesus breaks the bread that calls him into our experience.
He pours the wine of joy that helps us celebrate his sacrifice.
He comes to us in acts, symbols and signs that enrich us.
He awakens remembrance, binding past and present to the future.
He blesses this feast we share because he first shared it.
He places a family around us to share these precious things.

(162) Prayer of Dedication

May we proclaim Christ's death and rising,
Not only through the bread and wine, but in our fervour for justice
Wherever broken and betrayed are weeping for comfort;
In our concern and commitment to those who need to hear God's
    Word;
In our gifts, used by you and for you, in the building of your
    Kingdom.

(163) Prayer of Dismissal

Go with God, who sustains you with the Bread of Life, who
quenches your thirst with the wine that flows to bring you life, who
washes your feet as a friend who will never leave your side.

GOOD FRIDAY

Isaiah 52.13–53.12; Psalm 22; Hebrews 10.16–25 or
Hebrews 4.14–16; 5.7–9; John 18.1–19.42

UNFINISHED BUSINESS

Presentation

*Illustration: Darkness. You may choose to end the service by
extinguishing all the lights as the congregation leaves. Use the
presentation to prepare for and explore this symbolism more fully.
Turn off lights and light the church only with candles, and blow them
out one by one until all is dark. What do we feel about the dark?
What dangers in an unlit street? Evil deeds can go under cover; we
miss our footing and risk injury; everyday objects can seem
frightening and strange. When light is gone, darkness takes over.
When love dies on the cross, fear has free reign. But like waiting for
the sun to rise again, this is unfinished business!*

(164) Call to Worship

Isaiah 52.13–15 or Psalm 22.1–5

(165) Prayer of Adoration

God, your eternal power looks through the darkness to the light
  beyond:
Eternal God, though the darkness overwhelms us, we praise you.
Your eternal patience looks through the agony to the hope of glory:
Eternal God, though the agony terrifies us, we praise you.
Your eternal compassion looks through fears and doubts to the
  spark of renewal:
Eternal God, though fears and doubts grip us, we praise you.

(166) Prayer of Confession

*Play suitable music based on the Good Friday story. Allow plenty of
opportunity for confession in silence before concluding slowly with
the following prayer.*

Darkness: our selfishness has brought darkness into the lives of our
  sisters and brothers.
Darkness: our pride has brought darkness to our neighbours.

Darkness: our failure to burn with the light of your love has left us
   in darkness.
Forgive us that we have held the nails that were driven in so cruelly.
Forgive us that we have shaped the cross where you are bound.
Forgive us that we have often walked away, leaving you forsaken.
Silence
Through the darkness, we hear the words that lift us and bring us
   new hope:
'Father, forgive, for they do not know what they are doing.'

(167) Prayer of Thanksgiving

Thank you, Jesus, that you know us well enough to see what we
need, and that you had the love and courage to go to the place of our
healing.
Thank you, God of All.
Thank you, Jesus, that you were so in tune with the will of your
Father, yet chose to taste a moment of separation to draw nearer to
your mockers and murderers, to give us life.
Thank you, God of All.
Thank you, Jesus, that we will leave your house today under the
cloud of death, knowing you have snuffed out any dreams that you
would save yourself, yet that we can carry the seeds of hope in our
hearts for a glorious conclusion to this unfinished business.
Thank you, God of All.

(168) Prayer of Petition

Jesus, give us the patience to wait in the void of night, the vision to
   keep hope alive.
May we bring comfort to those who wait in darkness,
Who can see no safe place to plant their feet.
The curtain of the temple is torn in two:
Beckon us through to where you stand.
May we stand with the bereft and the bewildered,
To bring them your comfort until you arise.

(169) Prayer of Dedication

What can we do? **We can wait and watch.**
What can we say? **We can declare that the story is not over.**
What can we give? **We can give our all to the One who gave
   everything for us.**

What can we hope? **We can hope for joy after sorrow, comfort after tears, light after darkness, life after death.**

(170) Prayer of Dismissal

God has not forsaken us. His Spirit has not deserted us. Our Jesus is not defeated. The Spirit will draw near to comfort us. God will be faithful to walk with us. Our Jesus will rise again.

HOLY SATURDAY

Job 14.1–14 (or Lamentations 3.1–9; 19–24); Psalm 31.1–4, 15–16;
I Peter 4.1–8; Matthew 27.57–66 (or John 19.38–42)

SEALED BY STONE

Presentation

*Illustration: Prisons and chrysalises. Talk about the difference
between places where we have to stay. Prison; bars at the window,
guards to keep you in, held against your will. Is Jesus in prison in the
tomb? Is he held against his will? Look at the protective hard
chrysalis of a butterfly or moth. Draw out the contrast. The butterfly
cannot escape before its time has come. While it is inside, it is safe
from predators. But soon, at the right moment, it will burst out to a
new phase of life. Jesus, too, waits for the right moment to come back
to life. His death is real. It cannot be rushed. He is not there against
his will, but to fulfil the will of the Father.*

(171) Call to Worship

Job 14.13–15 or Lamentations 3.22–24

(172) Prayer of Adoration

Hope beyond hope, you are our God;
We come before you for we have no other consolation.
Driven into darkness where there seems to be no light,
We recognize your hand shaping the slow tread of these world-
    shattering events.
In you, Lord, we take refuge, let us never be put to shame.

Hope of the silent tomb, you are our God.
We adore you for all you are in life's darkest hours;
You stand with us, when human words fail, and your Word is all
    we can cling to.
We recognize your power even in absence and desolation.
In you, Lord, we take refuge, let us never be put to shame.

(173) Prayer of Petition

We sit in the darkness like the dead.
We do not know what to pray, we do not know what to do.
The hours hang heavy, and hope seems a mocking illusion.
Silence
The Lord is my portion, says my soul, so I will hope in him.

Our sorrow has drawn us into ourselves;
We look at our own resources, and lose all vision.
We do not know where to turn, we do not know whom to trust.
There seems only silence where we long to hear your voice.
Silence
The Lord is my portion, says my soul, so I will hope in him.

(174) Prayer of thanksgiving

God of deepest mystery, we have never met a mystery deeper than
  this,
That the sun can set and rise again without our Lord on earth.
We thank you that through mystery you turn us to the truth.

God of deepest love, we have never met a love deeper than this,
That when all seems bleak and cheerless, in limbo and out of focus,
You call to us across the distance of our shattered hope.
We thank you that through love, you turn the world upside down.

(175) Prayer of Dedication

When we are at the bottom of the pit, the only way is up.
When we have lost our confidence through despair,
The only way is onward.
Lord, we pledge ourselves to move upwards from this place.
Lord, we pledge ourselves to move onward with your strength.

(176) Prayer of Dismissal

If you feel too weary to walk: **we will let God carry us.**
If you feel too crushed to rise: **we will let God lift us.**
If you feel too empty to hope: **we will trust in God.**
Tomorrow is coming: **we open our hearts to await the God of
  tomorrow.**

EASTER DAY

Acts 10.34–43 (or Isaiah 65.17–25); Psalm 118.1–2, 14–24;
I Corinthians 15.19–26 (or Acts 10.34–43); John 20.1–18
(or Luke 24.1–12)

THIS IS THE DAY

Presentation

*Illustration: Butterfly: see Holy Saturday and recall the chrysalis.
Then show and talk about the butterfly. Things are no longer the
same. It has changed completely. Jesus has changed the whole world
by being raised to life. What is behind the change in the butterfly and
the change on Easter morning? God's creative, resurrection power.
What changes in our life because of Easter? How can we tell others
about this miracle?*

(177) Call to Worship

Psalm 118.1–2 or Isaiah 65.17–19 or the following:

This is the day that the Lord has made:
We will rejoice and be glad in it!
Alleluia! Christ is risen. **He is risen indeed! Alleluia!**

(178) Prayer of Adoration

O God, King of the Universe, we worship you.
Our joy is complete! Resurrection love has triumphed over death!
This is the Lord's doing! How marvellous to see it with our own
    eyes!
The Lord is my strength and my song:
And he has become my salvation!

O God, you have taken our sorrow
And turned it into joy beyond measure or imagining!
You have taken our fears and failure
And turned them into triumph that knows no bounds!
Not even death could hold on to Jesus;
The grave is empty and the cross witnesses to love's liberation.
The Lord is my strength and my song:
And he has become my salvation!

(179) Prayer of Thanksgiving

For rolling the stone away: **we thank you, living God.**
For weeping turned to dancing: **we thank you, living God.**
For our name spoken tenderly by Love: **we thank you, living God.**
For morning after the longest night: **we thank you, living God.**
For turning us topsy-turvy with joy: **we thank you, living God.**
For fragile trust held in reliable hands: **we thank you, living God.**
For a story beginning that has no end: **we thank you, living God.**

(180) Meditation

The garden seemed empty, drained of colour;
My heart was sick and the stubborn tears kept flowing.
I was glad it was still dark. Things could get no worse, but to have
    strangers staring,
Wondering what I had lost: Only my everything, my Lord, my
    Love, my Master!
Not content with his death, they had taken his body.
Not content with his suffering, they had to increase my own!
Then that strange waking dream of angels, my mind must be turning!
My eyes were swollen, but I was not mistaken.
A man, the gardener, loitering in the receding shadows.
'Leave me to grieve!' I wanted to scream. But the scream died in
    my throat.
I told him my story and he called me by my name: Mary.
Silence
The sun had come up.

(181) Prayer of Dedication

Gracious God, you have overwhelmed us with joy.
Nothing will ever be the same again.
May we live the change you have made in us.
May we live the love you have shown to us.
May we live the life you have won for us.

(182) Prayer of Dismissal

Now may the joy of the risen Lord, the mystery of Resurrection
power and the grace of the living God go with us as we bear the good
news to the world he has transformed. **Alleluia!**

SECOND SUNDAY OF EASTER

Acts 5. 27–32; Psalm 118.14–29 (or Psalm 150); Revelation 1. 4–8;
John 20.19–31

SEEING AND BELIEVING

Presentation
*Illustration: Optical illusions or pictures with ambiguities (like the
famous silhouette in which some see two faces looking at each other
while others will see a vase which appears to be framed by their
features). What do we see? Can we trust our eyes? Sometimes what
we see depends on what we expect to see. Thomas expected the Lord
to be dead. He couldn't believe without seeing the nail marks for
himself. We depend on our five senses for information. Touch was
important to Thomas as proof. Are there things we can believe
without seeing? What evidence do we need to believe in Jesus?*

(183) Call to Worship

*Psalm 118.14–16 or Psalm 150 using different voices, preferably
also some of the instruments mentioned!*

(184) Prayer of Adoration

God is the Lord: **he has made his light shine on us.**
Creator and Lover of the world, everywhere we can use our eyes to
    see your beauty:
The delicacy of the flower's secret heart, the smiling faces of the
    ones we love,
The sunlight on the foaming breakers,
And the telescope opening up a world of explosive new births
    among distant stars.
Yet you are much more than the evidence of creation.
God is the Lord: **he has made his light shine on us.**

God is the Lord: **he has made his light shine on us.**
Creator and Lover of the world, everywhere we can use our ears to
    hear your beauty:
The cry of a baby who has struggled to be born against the odds,
The symphony's dovetailing cathedral of sound or the drum and
    bass of modern music.

Yet you are much more than the evidence of creation.
God is the Lord: **he has made his light shine on us.**

(185) Prayer of Confession

Lord, we do not use the senses we have for your glory:
We have ignored the signs and signals given by those struggling to
    get our attention;
We have dulled our ears to the murmur of voices from lands where
    we have no vested interest;
We have refined our taste so we prefer foods that exploit and ruin
    poor labourers;
We have neglected to touch the textures and grains of the planet we
    are slowly killing;
We are out of touch with creation, except for our gain, for luxury
    or pleasure:
Forgive our wastefulness and ingratitude for all you have given.
From your bountiful mercy, Lord, put us back in touch and heal us
    for others' sake.

(186) Prayer of Thanksgiving

Read Acts 5.27–32

Active God, we thank you for the acts of your apostles,
Who obeyed you rather than human authority.
Thank you for their pioneering work in the early church,
Confronting first-century red tape
And finding ways of telling the world what love had done in Jesus.
Thank you that the message of Easter will never grow stale,
That their witness for you inspires your witnesses in every age.

(187) Payer of Dedication

Thomas took time to make sense of the evidence;
Then he declared boldly: 'My Lord and my God!'
May we from this day be bold to tell the world who you are:
Among the powerful who are threatened by your message, and may
    scorn us,
Among the powerless who are thirsty to redress the balance of
    injustice, and may overtake us,
Among our own who are so familiar with us they may find it hard
    to take us seriously.

In our words, in our actions, in our whole witness, may we declare:
My Lord and my God!

(188) Prayer of Dismissal

You have met the Risen, Living Christ here; do not imprison him in a silent heart and between closed lips, but go and make him known to your fellow travellers in the world.

THIRD SUNDAY OF EASTER

Acts 9.1–6 (7–20); Psalm 30; Revelation 5.11–14; John 21.1–19

MYSTERIOUS MEETINGS

Presentation

Illustration: Fishing. Play a game of fishing for paper fish with paper clips attached in a cardboard 'tank' which conceals them. First let people fish with rods of string; nothing is caught! Then fish with strings with small magnets attached to the end. What makes the difference to the success? Jesus acts as the magnet in the encounter with Paul on the Damascus Road, and for the disciples. Talk about life-changing encounters. Have we had our lives changed by events or by people? The Risen Christ draws people to him. How can we be 'magnets' for others to help them encounter him? The Gospel reading might make today suitable for a simple shared 'Prayer Breakfast' before the service.

(189) Call to Worship

Revelation 5.11–12 or Psalm 30.1–3

(190) Prayer of Adoration

Master of miracle and mystery, you come walking to us
On the beach of morning. We come before you at first light, to
    worship
The One who made heaven and earth and all that are in them.
You lift us up when life seems too pressing in its demands,
When nets are empty and spirits low.
You point us in the right direction when we walk on the wrong roads.
As we worship, make the scales fall from our eyes,
To see you as you are:
O Lord our God, we give you thanks forever.

(191) Prayer of Confession

Forgiving God, there are times when we have cast our nets
And felt so discouraged by what we have caught
We have despaired and stopped trying.
**Forgiving God, where we have gone wrong, show your healing
    mercy.**

There are times when you have shown us
Where there will be rich rewards for our labours,
And we have felt so inadequate that we have gone our own way
Ignoring your call, your gentle, persistent questioning.
**Forgiving God, where we have gone wrong, show your healing
mercy.**

(192) Prayer of Thanksgiving

We thank you, God of encounter, that you care for us
So much that when we run the other way, or get things hopelessly
wrong,
Still you come after us, letting us recognize you.
We praise you that you go on gently questioning us as you did Peter:
Do we love you?
Thank you, that our partial answers do not make you turn away,
But that you still go on, pressing as far as we can bear, no further.
Thank you for the opportunity of meeting you,
Wherever we may be, whoever we are.

(193) Prayer of Petition

On the road, you came to Paul,
When he was still breathing murder against your people.
You came in a flash that he could not ignore.
Come to us, Lord, in ways we cannot ignore.
You came to the disciples on the lake,
Among all the familiar things of their experience,
The nets, the fish, the morning sun on the water,
And you broke the bread and fish to feed them.
Come to us, Lord, in familiar ways.
You came to Peter after breakfast,
With questions and commissions of love:
You touched the deep places of commitment,
And prepared him for the journey.
Come to us, Lord, in ways of love and challenge.

(194) Prayer of Dismissal

Go in the strength of your risen Lord, to meet him in unexpected
places, to see him in unexpected people, and to let him deepen in you
that love that embraces all the world.

FOURTH SUNDAY OF EASTER

Acts 9.36–43; Psalm 23; Revelation 7.9–17; John 10.22–30

THE VOICE OF THE SHEPHERD

Presentation
Illustration: Shepherds: Show pictures or video clips of shepherds from the Holy Land. Talk about our stereotypes of shepherds. Brainstorm and list the images that come to mind. Explain how real shepherds had personal knowledge of each of their flock and knew them by name. Does our church make us feel nameless and remote? Does society do so with others? Or is there the same sense of being known personally? Are there changes we need to make? Jesus promised: 'No one will snatch them out of my hand.' Which things, people or situations might try to 'snatch' us from Jesus?

(195) Call to Worship

Psalm 23.1–2 or Revelation 7.9–10

(196) Prayer of Adoration

Shepherd Saviour, we worship you, right where we are.
Your goodness and mercy follow us all our days,
And here in your house, we rejoice to meet you.
Shepherd Saviour, you know us by name,
Watching us with protective love that will not leave us to wander
While we trust in you.
Shepherd Saviour, we worship you, saving and suffering One.
You comfort us when tears and troubles come,
Leading us to restful places to renew our strength, which comes
    from you.
Fill our worship with the warmth of your caring and joy.

(197) Prayer of Confession

God, we are remote from shepherds and those who herd the flocks;
But care is something we can understand, and our hearts leap to hear
our names called in love and compassion. We know that nothing can
snatch us from your hand, Loving Lord, but we want to confess the
things in our lives that block our ears at times to your distinct,
welcome voice:

hard-hearted attitudes and lack of listening;
love of self and intolerance of those who are difficult or just
   different;
ambition and a love of the status it gives us with the world;
waywardness and a drive to be independent, even of you.
Bring us back into the circle of your healing and forgiveness. Call
us again into the fold we can call home.

(198) Prayer of Thanksgiving

To the Shepherd Provider whose guiding eye is on the whole
   universe,
Keeping the stars in place and all people in his care:
We give thanks from the fold of God's love.
To the Shepherd King, who laid down his life for the sheep,
Who calls us by name and makes our wellbeing his care:
We give thanks from the fold of God's love.
To the Shepherd Spirit, who guides with her eye,
And lives in our hearts, influencing with a quiet unfailing
   compassion:
We give thanks from the fold of God's love.

(199) Prayer of Petition

Give us the compassion to speak with your tones of love, when
   others are longing to hear themselves called by name.
Give us the devotion of Tabitha to her craft, that whatever skills we
   have, we may perfect them in you and use them for others.
Give us the steady faith to believe your promises and live by your
   power.

(200) Prayer of Dedication

In the things we do and the way we do them:
May the voice of the Shepherd be heard.
In the words we speak and the way we say them:
May the voice of the Shepherd be heard.
In the gifts we have and the way we use them:
May the voice of the Shepherd be heard.
In the whole of our lives and the way we live them:
May the voice of the Shepherd be heard.

(201) Prayer of Dismissal

May we walk with the Shepherd, in earshot of his calling, in the pasture of his peace and the enfolding of his love.

FIFTH SUNDAY OF EASTER

Acts 11.1–18; Psalm 148; Revelation 21.1–6; John 13. 31–35

A NEW COMMANDMENT

Presentation

Illustration: Symbols of love: hearts and flowers, cupids, chocolate boxes with fancy bows, wedding rings. Talk about how we show love to each other. Read the new commandment. What was new about it? What is different about the way Jesus loves us? What evidence is there of this kind of love? What symbols of this love would we choose? Can people tell we are Jesus' disciples? How?

(202) Call to Worship

Psalm 148.1–6
The congregation could be encouraged to call out 'Praise him' each time the phrase occurs, perhaps accompanied by a simple action, such as raising hands to heaven.

(203) Prayer of Adoration

Praise the Lord, who has made everything in heaven and on earth!
Alleluia! Praise the Lord from earth and heaven!
Praise the Lord, who has made things we see, hear and touch every
    day:
The waving hands of our friends, the shout of laughter at a funny joke, the softness of our pets' fur and their cold wet noses, the special pattern of the spider's web and the crunch of toast at breakfast.

The congregation could be encouraged beforehand to make a list of everyday things in creation they enjoy. These can be added to the prayer by them or by the leader.

Praise the Lord, who has made everything in heaven and on earth!
Alleluia! Praise the Lord from earth and heaven!
Praise the Lord who has made things we can only wonder about:
The whirling galaxies circling through astonishing distances, the electrical impulses in our nerves and brains, the force of gravity tying things down and the unseen energy keeping planes in flight.

The congregation could add other mysteries.

Praise the Lord, who has made everything in heaven and on earth!
Alleluia! Praise the Lord from earth and heaven!

(204) Prayer of Confession

Lord, you told us to love one another and we ended up quarrelling
again:
Forgive us, and help us to keep your commandment.
You taught us to trust God and we thought we knew even better:
Forgive us, and help us to keep your commandment.
You showed us new ways and we felt more comfortable with the
old ones:
Forgive us, and help us to keep your commandment.
Silence
You show us a new heaven and a new earth: may we now live in
your forgiveness and put off old ways for your sake.

(205) Prayer of Thanksgiving

A new heaven and a new earth!
What a joy to hear your promise that the best is yet to come!
You promise us a time when death will not be the surest thing in
life any more;
You promise us a time when you will wipe our tears away forever;
You promise us a time when pain and mourning will not make us
sad.
See! God is making all things new!
Praise to the God who goes on creating!

(206) Prayer of Petition or Dedication

Alpha and Omega, A to Z of our life,
Give us the courage to believe in the changes you can make, and to
choose them for ourselves and our loved ones.
Give us the wisdom to realize the changes we can make, and to go
with you to those who are suffering, sad or discouraged, to those who
are on the wrong end of an unfair deal in life, and make a difference.

(207) Prayer of Dismissal

See, God is making all things new!
We go into the world to live out his new commandment!

SIXTH SUNDAY OF EASTER

Acts 16.9–15; Psalm 67; Revelation 21.10, 22–22.5;
John 14.23–29 or John 5.1–9

SPIRIT OF PEACE

Presentation
Illustration: Get the congregation to make as loud a noise as possible, and then call for complete peace. Who felt embarrassed or upset by noise in church and who enjoyed it? The world can be a noisy place. List things that make noises that upset us. Write this as: 'We like peace from . . .' We all have different needs for peace in our lives. What do we imagine is different about this peace that Jesus promises in the Holy Spirit?

(208) Call to Worship

Psalm 67.1–2 or 3–5

(209) Prayer of Adoration

God of Glory, we turn to you with adoration.
You have made a world full of sounds and noises that greet us everywhere: pops and bangs, bubbling and squeaking, rattles and hums, whispers and giggles, scraping and singing, moaning and murmuring, barking and chirruping:
We adore you, God of Sound and Silence.

You have made a world with opportunities for peace: the deepest oceans where the fish and aquatic animals swim through the darkness with their secret life unlit by the sun, the mountain tops with their heads in the clouds, the still before the tornado in the eye of the storm, the hours of darkness in the night when some of us are sleeping, but the work goes on:
We adore you, God of Sound and Silence.

(210) Prayer of Confession

For all the times we have had chances and wasted them:
God of new chances, have mercy and set us free.
For all the times we have been shown love and have been nasty in return:

God of new chances, have mercy and set us free.
For all the times we have spoilt somebody's peace by pestering:
God of new chances, have mercy and set us free.

(211) Prayer of Petition

Read Acts 16.9–15

Lydia was a worshipper of God:
Give us a new joy in worshipping our Maker and Lord.
She listened eagerly to what Paul and his friends were saying:
Give us ears to hear your word wherever it is spoken.
She was a dealer in purple cloth:
**Give us a joy in our work and play and may we do everything
in your name.**
She opened her heart and her home:
Give us hospitality to open ourselves to others and to you.

(212) Prayer of Thanksgiving

Thank you, Lord, that when you went away you left your Spirit as
our Advocate, to speak up for us and to teach and remind us what
you would want us to do.
Thank you that you left with us your peace that is like nothing
earth can give us. Help us to live in your peace when we feel
overworked or anxious, upset or scared.
Thank you that you taught us about your Father, and helped us to
understand him by the things you did in your life

(213) Prayer of Dismissal

Go in the peace of the Creator who holds you when everything seems
chaos: go in the peace of Christ who accompanies you into noisy
places: go in the peace of the Holy Spirit who whispers deep within
you words of comfort and brings you home.

ASCENSION DAY

Acts 1.1–11; Psalm 47 (or Psalm 93); Ephesians 1.15–23;
Luke 24.44–53

RETURNING TO GLORY

Presentation
*Illustration: a return ticket for bus or train. Talk about places visited
that you always want to go back to. How does it feel when you are
away from home for a while? Is it good to get home after a holiday?
We need to hang on to our return portion of a plane ticket if we travel
to some countries, to show we are not permanent residents there.
Jesus was returning to his Father after his time on earth. Did Jesus
hang on to part of his heavenly life when he came to earth? What
things might have been difficult for Jesus, being a citizen of heaven
and earth? What might the disciples have felt about Jesus'
Ascension?*

(214) Call to Worship

Psalm 47.1–2 or Psalm 93.1–2

(215) Prayer of Adoration

God of heaven and earth, you are our King, reigning over all the
universe with power and justice.
Clap your hands, all you peoples; shout to God with a cry of joy.
You raised Jesus back to the glory from which he came, dazzling at
his homecoming, leaving us amazed at the love which first brought
him to live our life on earth.
Clap your hands, all you peoples; shout to God with a cry of joy.
Your power looks through limitations to possibilities; your love
looks through failures and death to the purposes you have been
shaping since the foundation of the world.
Clap your hands, all you peoples; shout to God with a cry of joy.
You have lifted our eyes to the cross, to see hope through our tears;
You have lifted our eyes to the sky, to see Christ's glory through
our disbelief.
Clap your hands, all you peoples; shout to God with a cry of joy.

(216) Prayer of Confession

Forgive us, Ascended Lord, when we stand so long gaping at the sky where you have gone up to glory, that we fail to turn our eyes back to your world, where so many people starve through our greed, weep through our selfishness, die through our neglect.
Ascended Lord, we are renewed by your forgiveness.
Forgive us, when we spend so long with our heads in the clouds, that we neglect your work at grass roots level, not wanting to get our hands dirty with things you have asked us to do.
Ascended Lord, we are renewed by your forgiveness.

(217) Prayer of Thanksgiving

This prayer could be linked to the Lord's Prayer
The Kingdom is yours, Ascended Saviour.
We thank you that Creation's power has put everything under your
    feet,
That you are above every name that is named in this age and the
    age to come.
Thank the God of the Kingdom.
The power is yours, Ascended Saviour.
We thank you that you use your power to liberate and heal us,
That you give us power by the Holy Spirit to challenge the powers
    of the world.
Thank the God of All Power.
The glory is yours, Ascended Saviour.
We thank you that you have ascended to the glory that is rightly
    your own.
We thank you and ask that we may reflect that glory to a world that
    revels in its own empty glory.
Thank the God of All Glory.

(218) Prayer of Petition

Open our eyes to see your glory and prepare ourselves for your
    coming.
Open up our closed minds to expect new truths to dawn on us from
    the scriptures.
As you patiently explained your place in God's plan to the first
    disciples,
so we ask that you may help us to realize our place in the plans you
    are making and to act faithfully on what you show us.

(219) Prayer of Dedication

As we celebrate your ascension to the pinnacle of creation,
Reigning as King of earth and heaven in glory,
Take what we are and raise us to what we can be:
We will mirror your glory to a waiting world.

(220) Prayer of Dismissal

May the Kingdom, the power and the glory of the Ascended Jesus
keep your eyes fixed on eternity, your feet grounded on certain hope,
and your life centred on God, as you live and work for him.

SEVENTH SUNDAY OF EASTER

Acts 16.16–34; Psalm 97; Revelation 22.12–14, 16–17, 20–21;
John 17.20–26

ONE IN LOVE

Presentation
*Illustration: Play the game where a group facing inwards in a circle
join hands at random and then attempt to extricate themselves to
form a ring without loosing their grip. They may need to struggle and
step over arms and legs! Read John 17.22–23. Are there difficulties
in us 'being one' as disciples of Jesus? In the game, the more agile
may have needed to do more to help the less mobile. Others needed
to allow those close to pull them around. Give and take was needed
to work as one body. What efforts do we need to make as Christians
to help one another to live 'as one'?*

(221) Call to Worship

Psalm 97.11–12 or the following:

The Spirit of God and the church in her joy as Jesus' bride say:
   Come!
And let everyone who hears say: **Come!**
To all who are thirsty, the Lord says: **Come!**
Let us all come together to worship the Lord our God!

(222) Prayer of Adoration

Startling God, all creation reveals your mighty hand: the masses of
islands that each have their place in the oceans, the clouds and the
darkness that speak of the shadow side of our world, the mystery
and the unfathomable, known only to you:
We celebrate you, God who startles and satisfies!
Breathtaking God, in lightning and hurricane, your unstoppable
nature is seen; in gusts and gales your world expresses your power;
yet greater still than your power in nature is the glory revealed in
Jesus. In him power that could shatter stone cradles us with a
mother's attentive care; force that could erupt the volcano comes to
us with a still small voice and the eyes of a child:
We celebrate you, God who startles and satisfies!

Measureless God, you are beyond yet ever close; in the Spirit you come to interpret yourself to our limited vision. You satisfy us with attention to every detail, and even in chaos your awesome rhythm can be traced. The grace and the glory are yours, and we live to adore you!

We celebrate you, God who startles and satisfies!

(223) Prayer of Confession

Lord, you prayed that we would be completely one in love, as you and your Father are one.

You often find us struggling against one another, divided, sulky, defensive of our own identity, unwilling to share or compromise.

Lord, have patience, and wash our guilt away.

You said that you gave us your glory, the glory that you were given by God.

You meant the world to recognize God in us, but you know that the tired and tarnished face we reveal to the world leaves most people wondering who you are and what could be glorious about our hope.

Lord, have patience, and wash our guilt away.

(224) Meditation

Read Acts 16.25–28

Lord, I need to be shaken; shaken out of this stupor that imprisons and diminishes me; fears, fantasies and illusions . Even as the hymns are sung and prayers are said at midnight, there is no light in my heart but heaviness. Chains wrap me round and round like bindweed, crushing the flower of hope in me. I cannot lift my head, even to see the bars at the window. Yet I am the jailer. Weighed down by my own keys I am rooted to the dungeon. Then a tremor, distant at first. I look up, startled and out of my depth. Out of the depth, I meet compassion in the eyes of a prisoner and the strange uncalled-for confidence of the songs in the icy night. I shrink from them, but now every stone is shaking. I lose my footing. I am found.

(225) Prayer of Petition

Jesus, give us the complete unity that strengthens us to do your work;
Give us the glimpse of your glory that is like a postcard of home;
Give us your love to equip us, free us and send us out in your name.

(226) Prayer of Dedication

We can give you nothing but what you have given us,
We can show you nothing but what you have revealed to us;
We can hope for nothing but what you have won for us:
**May we give you our all, show out your glory and hope for
  salvation.**

(227) Prayer of Dismissal

Let us go, unbound by the chains that have imprisoned us, bound to
one another in love and bound for the glory of the Lord Jesus Christ:
In the name of the Maker, the Saviour and the Spirit, we go !

PENTECOST

Acts 2.1–21(or Genesis 11.1–9); Psalm 104.24–34, 35b;
Romans 8.14–17 (or Acts 2.1–21); John 14.8–17 (25–27)

TONGUES OF TRANSFORMING FIRE

Presentation
*Illustration: Babel: Prepare to have a dozen different voices read
unrelated passages from books, newspapers, popular songs, etc,
loudly at the same time. Encourage the rest to try to make sense of
anything they hear. Remind them about the Tower of Babel. Has
anyone tried to learn another language, or gone abroad unarmed
with anything but phrasebook basics? Communication can be
difficult. Talk about the experience at Pentecost. How does the Spirit
reverse things? Now get the same voices to read Acts 2.1–21
together, in choral speaking.*

(228) Call to Worship

Psalm 104.33–34 with the response:

The Lord has sent his Spirit, and renewed the face of the earth.

(229) Prayer of Adoration

Holy Spirit, we adore you, rushing into our experience on this day
    of Pentecost!
Creative Spirit, we adore you and welcome you in to fire our
    imaginations in new directions.
Spirit of Communication, we adore you, and ask you to be the
    language of love between us.
Spirit of Healing, we adore you, coming to mend rifts and jump
    ravines to join us.
Spirit of Joy, we adore you, fluttering through our worship with the
    wings of a dove.
Spirit of Adoption, we adore you, as you gather us together and
    gather us in to God.

(230) Prayer of Confession

Merciful God, we make our confession to you by the power of the
　　Spirit:
When we have used our experience of your Spirit to make others
　　feel excluded and inadequate;
When we have used our own fears as windbreaks to resist the
　　breath of life blowing in our lives;
When we have used our words to confuse and kick over the traces
　　of our own confusion;
When we have stamped out the fire of the spirit to avoid being set
　　alight for you;
May the Advocate speak in our hearts to reveal all we hide before
　　God:
Silence
Lord, what we have confessed, we know you will forgive for Jesus'
　　sake.
Refresh us, remake us, set us on fire with your love.

(231) Prayer of Thanksgiving

For pouring out on your church the resources it needs to burn with
　　the flame of compassion, to be replenished by the oil of faith and
　　fanned by the wings of the dove of peace:
We thank you, generous God.
For filling us to overflowing from the spring of the Spirit,
　　cascading into the lives of those you touch with miracle and
　　mystery:
We thank you, generous God.
For exploding into dulled hearts with the fizz and bounce of
　　freedom, for bursting the bubble of pomposity with laughter and
　　gentle joy:
We thank you, generous God.

(232) Prayer of Petition

On hearts weary with waiting: **Pour out your Spirit.**
On imaginations jaded with mediocrity: **Pour out your Spirit.**
On travellers worn down by trudging: **Pour out your Spirit.**
On all your people, longing for renewal: **Pour out your Spirit.**

(233) Prayer of Dedication

**Lord we open our lives afresh today, to the baptism of your
Holy Spirit;
We are open to be licked by the gentle flames of healing;
We are open to be washed in rains from a new horizon;
We are open to be inspired by the rainbow of Pentecost
blessings;
Unite us to be reborn in the radiance of your grace.**

(234) Prayer of Dismissal

May we walk now with wings on our feet, to tread in the path of
God's mercy, to dance with the risen Saviour and to skip to the
Spirit's tune of grace.

TRINITY SUNDAY

Proverbs 8.1–4, 22–31; Psalm 8; Romans 5.1–5; John 16.12–15

CREATOR, SAVIOUR AND SPIRIT

Presentation

Illustration: Celtic knot. This or another symbol used to talk about the Trinity, such as the cup, stream and spring. Talk about the limitations of any visual or symbolic representation of the Trinity. Point out that the Bible does not try to make a neat formula. How do we know God? As Creator? As Jesus? As Spirit? Some answers may well touch on all three! All our experience of God comes from encounter, not an equation!

(235) Call to Worship

Psalm 8.1 or the following:

Let us praise God as our Creator: **Let us praise our God together.**
Let us praise God as our Saviour: **Let us praise our God together.**
Let us praise God as our Guide and Advocate: **Let us praise our God together.**

(236) Prayer of Adoration

God of Mystery, you make yourself known in our world as the Creator. You have not left the universe to tick along like abandoned clockwork, singing the song of the spheres in the dark. You hold everything in the wise hands of a parent, tending and cherishing all you have made. You make everything your precious business, from the neon flash of the fish in deep water to the complex beat of the human heart; from families of primates and birds of paradise socializing under the thick canopy of the rainforest, to the spitting of the llama high on a mountain peak.
God of Mystery, we worship you as Creator.

God of Mystery, you make yourself known in our world through Jesus; you are not remote or indifferent, but you lived our life for love of us, to set us free from death and sorrow. You draw close to us as we call on you, urging us on to abundant life through the cross that stands empty. You teach us as you teach your sisters and brothers in every age, and we sit at your feet to be soothed or strengthened.
God of Mystery, we worship you as Christ our Lord.

God of Mystery, you make yourself known in our world as the Spirit, blowing through dead ideas like a light going on in heaven, inspiring and enabling. You live in our hearts, transforming us from the inside, turning us inside out and then refreshing us with your peace.
God of mystery, we worship you as the Holy Spirit.

(237) Prayer of Confession

United God, we confess we are a mass of contradictions.
We blow hot and cold, we are two-faced,
We tell different stories to different people to suit ourselves.
We have mood swings, fads and phases,
Following new fashions and changing to please our friends.
We look into your face: God you are Trinity, God you are One.
Lord, there is no contradiction in you; you are not three-faced!
You are Love. Trusting that love to forgive our fragmented values
    and our mixed up ways,
We come before you to ask forgiveness.
Silence
Out of our brokenness, you make us whole again.

(238) Prayer of Thanksgiving

For the protecting, providing hand of our Creator, nourishing and
    nurturing,
We give our thanks: **we give our thanks with joyful hearts.**
For the courage and compassion of Christ, sacrificing and regaining
    a Kingdom for us,
We give our thanks: **we give our thanks with joyful hearts.**
For the refreshing sweep of the Holy Spirit over stagnant waters,
    stirring us up,
We give our thanks: **we give our thanks with joyful hearts.**

(239) Prayer of Dedication

Let us dedicate ourselves to the Lord our God:
**Lord, we dedicate ourselves afresh: to rejoice in complexity, to
act with simplicity, to meet you wherever you reveal yourself in
all your threefold grace.**

(240) Prayer of Dismissal

We know that we are justified by faith, that we have peace through
our Lord Jesus Christ, and that God's love has been poured into our
hearts through the Holy Spirit that has been given to us.

SUNDAY BETWEEN 29 MAY AND 4 JUNE INCLUSIVE

(if after Trinity Sunday. Ninth Sunday in Ordinary Time)

I Kings 18.20–21 (22–29) 30–39; and Psalm 96 or I Kings 8.22–23, 41–43; and Psalm 96.1–9; Galatians 1.1–12; Luke 7.1–10

EXTRAORDINARY FAITH

Presentation

Illustration: use one of the trust-building exercises either where one person is led by another over a short obstacle course, or 'falls' blindfolded into a group and is carried by them. This takes great trust on the part of the one who cannot see. What is involved in faith and trust in another person or group? What do we risk? Do we need to trust ourselves first? Highlight how extraordinary is the trust of the centurion. He knows his own limitations. He does not even need Jesus to visit him. Sometimes risky faith and trust are needed for God's work to be done.

(241) Call to Worship

Psalm 96.1–3 or 4–6

(242) Prayer of Adoration

Lord of risks and surprises, you are God of an astounding universe.
You are worthy of a new song and we join together to sing it.
For great is the Lord: **and greatly to be praised.**
Lord of hopes and heartbreaks, you are the just judge;
You judge the world with righteousness and your people with your
    truth.
For great is the Lord: **and greatly to be praised.**
Lord of the 'thumbs up' and the question mark, you are alongside
    your children
In every situation, joyful or hair-raising, you never let us down.
For great is the Lord: **and greatly to be praised.**

(243) Prayer of Confession

We lay down at your feet, pardoning God, all our failures and lack
of faith.
We come to ask your mercy for all we have done wrong.
Sometimes we meant to do it, sometimes we were looking the other
way,
Sometimes we did not try our best, sometimes our pride got in the
way.
Sometimes we broke our limits, sometimes we stamped on
another's dreams.
But we gather up the petals we have plucked from the flower of
chances,
And let you scatter them on the wind of your mercy.
They are lost forever.
Silence
And as we look in our hands, we find Jesus has placed there a
perfect new flower,
Its petals as yet unruffled and without blemish, new chances, a new
beginning.
We are pardoned. We pray for the wisdom to walk a new way with
you.

(244) Prayer of Thanksgiving

Read Galatians 1.1–12

Thanks for the gospel that Paul proclaimed,
His conviction that kept on spreading the wonderful news about
Jesus.
Thanks for new opportunities to share the good news as he did,
That nothing but the truth was good enough.
May we never be satisfied with half-truths that might confuse those
who hear us.
Thanks for all the ways we can learn about you in the modern world:
For talks in church, for games and puzzles, for programs on the
computer and programmes on television;
For musicals, hymns and choruses, for action songs, books and
charts.
Most of all we thank you for the joy of discovering you for ourselves.

(245) Prayer of Petition

We know our limits: **Stretch our limits and feed our faith.**
We know our failings: **Forgive our mistakes and lead us forward.**
We know you can do anything, but are sometimes scared to let you:
Teach us to join in with the fun and walk the tightrope with you, hand in hand.

(246) Prayer of Dedication

We will rely on you, where once we held back in the shadows.
We will take risks with you, letting you show your power.
We will have faith in you, however weak and small it starts.
We give our lives to you, for they are not safe anywhere else.

(247) Prayer of Dismissal

Galatians 1.3–5

SUNDAY BETWEEN 5 AND 11 JUNE INCLUSIVE

(if after Trinity Sunday. Tenth Sunday in Ordinary Time)

I Kings 17.8–16 (17–24) and Psalm 146 or I Kings 17.17–24 and Psalm 30; Galatians 1.11–24; Luke 7.11–17

LIFE CHANGING POWER

Presentation
Illustration: Modern testimonies of people whose lives have been changed by meeting Christ. This will be most effective if shared by someone in the local congregation or community. Contrast before and after the encounter. What changed? Did others notice? Did the first effects wear off a little in time? Try setting up a mock interview with Paul based on the things he says in Galatians 1.11–24. What might be the attitude of others to such a dramatic turnabout? Talk about the widow of Nain and her son. How would their lives change after their meeting with Jesus?

(248) Call to Worship

Psalm 146.1–2 , 5–10 or Psalm 30.4–5, 11–12

(249) Prayer of Adoration

Praise the Lord, O my soul!
I will praise the Lord as long as I live!
Compassionate God, you are committed to the world you have
    created.
You watch out for the vulnerable ones who are bowed down and
    broken.
Your loving kindness goes beyond all we could deserve.
Praise the Lord, O my soul!
I will praise the Lord as long as I live!

Compassionate God, you do not give up on anything you have
    nursed and nurtured.
You look after the stranger and the widow
And you are a loving parent to those who have nobody else to care
    for them.

Praise the Lord, O my soul!
I will praise the Lord as long as I live!

(250) Prayer of confession

Loving God, we aren't always very good with people,
Not when they are in real need.
Other people's tears embarrass us, almost more than breaking down
 in public.
Forgive us when we shrink away from saying a word of comfort,
Just to let someone know they are not alone.
Forgive us when we go babbling on and saying too much,
Or when we lack the courage to risk saying nothing.
When we make light of others' pain, or try to shut them up
Because we want them to comfort us instead.

(251) Prayer of Petition

Increase our willingness to be changed, patient God,
Like Paul on the road, or the widows at Zarephath and Nain,
Who let Elijah and Jesus in to change death into life.
How can sorrow turn to dancing unless we let you in?
Give us greater expectations, and the faith that looks to a different
 dawn.

(252) Prayer of Dedication

Where can we go with what Jesus has shown us?
We will walk in his life-changing power.
What can we do with the things he has taught us?
We will act with his life-changing power.
How can we share what our Jesus has given us?
We will tell of his life-changing power.

(253) Prayer of Dismissal

The Lord goes with us, to bless our journeying with his presence, to
honour our faith in him with gifts of wonder and to change our lives
by his dynamic power.

SUNDAY BETWEEN 12 AND 18 JUNE INCLUSIVE

(if after Trinity Sunday. Eleventh Sunday in Ordinary Time)

I Kings 21.1–10, (11–14), 15–21a and Psalm 5.1–8 or
II Samuel 11.26–12.10, 13–15 and Psalm 32; Galatians 2.15–21;
Luke 7.36–8.3

LAYING DOWN THE LAW

Presentation
*Illustration: Signs and laws: Highway Code, 'keep off the grass' etc.
The law is everywhere! Do such laws help us or just make us nervous
or rebellious? We can do what the law says (paying tax etc.) or just
avoid breaking it (staying off grass). Which laws do we remember
from the Bible? Read Galatians 2.15–21. Jesus' way is not a set of
rules (though Moses' commandments all help to make life run
smoothly in society) but a freedom and an inner conviction. The
woman in Luke 7.36–8.3 has sinned by law, but acts in love.*

(254) Call to Worship
Psalm 5.7–8 or Psalm 32.1

(255) Prayer of Adoration

Lord whose law is love, you have made a world of choices.
The sun comes up over the horizon every day, the moons orbit their
    stars,
But to humans you give the luxury of making decisions,
Choices of what to wear and eat, and endless options of choosing
    right over wrong.
Loving God, we adore you.
Lord whose law is just, you have given us pointers and guidelines,
Not to trip or truss us up or to mummify our wills in regulations.
Rather you help us in the bewildering maze of free will,
Showing which paths are safe and lead to life.
Loving God, we adore you.

(256) Prayer of Confession

We are sorry, God who forgives.
We think we have done enough to get a tick in the right box.
We have not broken any law. No security camera has caught us
    stealing.
We have not murdered or mugged or even walked on the grass.
We even cleared up after the dog.
But we are sorry: we have broken the law of love.
We have not gone the extra mile, or greeted you with the joy
That smashes jars of perfume and kisses your feet.
We have not actively done anything more than was required.
Sometimes, even for your dear sake, we have not actively done
    anything.
Forgive us, in your mercy, and grant us the freedom of a fresh start.

(257) Prayer of Petition

Lord Jesus, you saw the difference between the judgmental attitude
of the Pharisee who said: 'She is a sinner' and the act of love
which went leaping and escaping the narrowness of legalism.
Give us the discernment to understand your law and live in your
    freedom.
Give us the love that runs to you with genuine adoration.

(258) Prayer of Thanksgiving

Thank you, God, that you instruct us, and do not leave everything
    to chance:
that you have chosen a way for us that is better than we could
    choose,
that you have promised to guide us with your eye,
that you do not want to lead us like mules with a bridle;
But that you give us understanding to work things out with the
    Spirit's help.

(259) Prayer of Dedication

The Lord is our hiding place, our rock and our refuge:
We will walk in safety, guided by his eye.
Not by doing the works of the law will we be justified:
We will walk by faith and believe in Jesus Christ.

(260) Prayer of Dismissal

Have faith in your Maker and walk in his grace; have faith in Christ
and walk in his love; have faith in the Spirit and walk in her power.
Your faith has saved you: go in peace.

SUNDAY BETWEEN 19 AND 25 JUNE INCLUSIVE

(if after Trinity Sunday. Twelfth Sunday in Ordinary Time)

I Kings 19.1–4, (5–7), 8–15a and Psalms 42 and 43 or Isaiah 65.1–9 and Psalm 22.19–28; Galatians 3.23–29; Luke 8.26–39

CLOTHED IN CHRIST

Presentation
Illustration: Uniforms: uniformed organizations can talk about changes in their own dress code, or let nurses, police, etc. show their working outfits. What do such clothes say about us? What do they say about the job we do and its demands? Read Galatians 3.23–29. What does it mean to be clothed in Christ? How can others recognize Christ in us? Talk about school uniforms helping to disguise differences in parental income (though be sensitive that this is not entirely true when designer trainers can accompany the basic kit!). Paul talks about breaking down barriers between slave and free, etc.

(261) Call to Worship

Psalm 42.1–2 or Psalm 22.27–28

(262) Prayer of Adoration

Trustworthy Father, you are glorious in all creation.
We come before you to worship you and learn about you,
To sing your praises with one voice and one heart.
We gather to sing your praises.

Trustworthy Christ, your words and your way of life always tell the
    same story.
We can trust you never to betray our confidence or shatter our hope.
You widen our horizons and throw new light into dark corners.
We gather to sing your praises.

Trustworthy Spirit, we depend on you to refresh us when we are
    weary.
Like deer that are thirsty for a stream of clear water,
We come to you to eagerly and open ourselves to your gift of life.
We gather to sing your praises.

(263) Prayer of Confession

Read Luke 8.26–39

Healing God, the man whom Jesus healed was sent home to declare
   how much you had done for him.
We confess we would often rather go racing off in a new direction
Than go home to those who know us to witness to them.
The man begged to follow Jesus where he was going,
But that was not his calling.
Healing God, we do not always listen to your call to go where you
   need us.
When it is not glamorous or rewarding or comfortable, we shy away.
We think nobody will know the difference.
Take and heal our disobedience.
Silence
Now we clothe ourselves in you and live to your glory.

(264) Prayer of Petition

We look at the dirty rags of our good intentions, and we pray:
Clothe us in Christ.
We feel shame at the threadbare fabric of our excuses, and we pray:
Clothe us in Christ.
We dress ourselves up in so many disguises, and we pray:
Clothe us in Christ.
We take off our old coats of selfishness and pride, and we pray:
Clothe us in Christ.

(265) Prayer of Dedication

**Lord, we dedicate ourselves to being spent only in the ways you
   lead us,**
To being refreshed only by the soft, healing breath of your Spirit,
**To being clothed only in Christ, that the world may recognize
   him in us**
And want to put on their party clothes, too!

(266) Prayer of Dismissal

Clothed in Christ, walk on knowing you are part of a great company,
dressed to celebrate a Creator who made you, a Saviour who loves
you and a Spirit who abides with you in all the days to come.

(267) Prayer of Dismissal

Now we are all children of God, through faith in Jesus Christ, and we go clothed in him to do his work in the world.

SUNDAY BETWEEN 26 JUNE AND 2 JULY INCLUSIVE

(Thirteenth Sunday in Ordinary Time)

II Kings 2.1–2, 6–14 and Psalm 77.1–2, 11–20 or
I Kings 19.15–16, 19–21 and Psalm 16; Galatians 5.1, 13–25;
Luke 9.51–62

TRUE FREEDOM

Presentation

Illustration: Play a game with two teams racing to wind newspapers or toilet rolls round a team member. Then get them to free themselves as quickly as they can. What does it mean to be free in Christ? Which things bind us in life? Read the list of works of the flesh from Galatians 5. Get the congregation to add others such as modern addictions and conflicts. Now look at the list of fruits of the Spirit. Do these help to free us from the items on the first list? One way to illustrate this is to drop ink into a glass of clean water as you mention each of the things that enslave, then pour in a jug of clean water (put a bowl underneath!) to symbolize the Spirit flushing them away until a clean glass remains.

(268) Call to Worship

Psalm 16.5–6, 7–8 or Psalm 77.13–15

(269) Prayer of Adoration

God of freedom, your ways are wonderful and we marvel
At everything your hand has made.
You go on astonishing us at every turn of life's journey,
By the bounty and richness of colour and the textures and rhythms
Of a universe teeming with unstoppable liveliness, singing its own
    song!
God of freedom, nothing can hold you in:
We worship you and welcome the freedom you bring.

God of freedom, in Jesus you have given us new life, new direction;
When we were straying out of earshot of your still, small voice,
You sent your only Son to lavish love on us.
We have done nothing to deserve you,

But as a loving Parent, you brought us to birth and will never give up on us.
God of freedom, nothing can hold you in:
We worship you and welcome the freedom you bring.

God of freedom, you sent the Holy Spirit to bring freedom flooding into our lives.
If we let your Spirit in, we find fruits that taste sweeter than anything on earth.
Love, joy and peace are the blessings that follow the buds and blossoms of meeting you.
Patience, kindness and generosity transform our friendships and make enemies friends.
Faithfulness, gentleness and self-control help us to live the life you have poured in,
That Jesus won for us on the cross that had itself to set him free once more!
God of freedom, nothing can hold you in:
We worship you and welcome the freedom you bring.

(270) Prayer of Confession

Read Luke 9. 51–62
Lord, you call us to follow, but we are too busy counting the cost:
Forgive us and help us get our priorities right.
You take our hand on the road, but sometimes we trip up from looking back:
Forgive us and help us to look forward with you.
You show us the way to freedom, but sometimes we tie ourselves in knots:
Forgive us and help us to let you unravel the tangles we make.
You take us seriously but sometimes we want you as an add-on extra:
Forgive us and help us to centre our lives on you.

(271) Prayer of Dismissal

God goes with us, to free us from all that binds us;
God goes with us, to free us to serve our neighbours;
God goes with us, to free us to live in his peace:
We go with God!

SUNDAY BETWEEN 3 AND 9 JULY INCLUSIVE

(Fourteenth Sunday in Ordinary Time)

II Kings 5.1–14 and Psalm 30 or Isaiah 66.10–14 and Psalm 66.1–9;
Galatians 6 (1–6), 7–16; Luke 10.1–11, 16–20

BOASTING IN CHRIST

Presentation
Illustration: Fishing tackle; show rod and fish. Talk about the traditional angling boasts, 'It was this big!', and each time the hands indicate bigger and bigger! What sort of things are we proud of? Do we boast to friends? Paul only wants to boast in the cross of Jesus. Jesus warns the seventy not to rejoice (boast) at the powers they can use, but only that they have a place with God. All we have (including big fish!) comes from God. Should this make us less eager to brag about ourselves? Write on paper fish cut-outs things God has done of which we can be proud.

(272) Call to Worship
Psalm 30.4–5 , 11–12 or Psalm 66.1–4

(273) Prayer of Adoration
We have come here to worship the God of all joy!
Sing the glory of God's name:
We sing the glory of his praise.
Everywhere we see the works that God is doing in his world,
His wonderful love to his people.
As a mother comforts her children, God has said:
'So will I comfort you.'
Sing the glory of God's name:
We sing the glory of his praise.

Jesus the Lord of sorrow and joy has come to earth to save us.
Because of what he carried for us, the cross, the insults, the sneering,
We are able to carry everything with his strength,
And we share the joy of knowing he has prepared a place for us
    with him forever.
Sing the glory of God's name:
We sing the glory of his praise.

(274) Prayer of Confession

Forgiving Friend, Lord God, listen to us as we bring our sins for
your healing.
We have ignored that fact that you have given us everything:
Our skills, our resources, our imaginations, our possessions.
We have pretended that it is all to our credit, and boasted to give
ourselves 'street cred'.
Forgive us, Lord God, and in your mercy save us.

Compassionate friend, Lord God, we have emphasized the gifts you
have given,
Using them to make ourselves seem powerful, clever and in control.
You are in control, Lord, and we are out of order.
Forgive us, Lord God, and in your mercy save us.

(275) Prayer of Petition

Jesus, you know us through and through; when we exaggerate and
say 'This big, honest!', 'This good, really!', you see our hearts,
and you know the truth.
You know we have nothing to boast about.
Give us the wisdom to boast only in Christ's cross.
You care about us, and when we get caught out in our boasting,
However ashamed we feel, however red our burning cheeks,
You cool us down, and help us learn our lesson.
Give us the wisdom to boast only in Christ's cross.

(276) Prayer of Dismissal

As we leave your house of nourishment, may we take with us the
strength from feeding on your Word, to help us help others, not
through our cleverness or by our deserving, but through the victory
of the Cross, the wisdom of the Spirit and the love that binds us all
to God.

SUNDAY BETWEEN 10 AND 16 JULY INCLUSIVE

(Fifteenth Sunday in Ordinary Time)

Amos 7.7–17 and Psalm 82 or Deuteronomy 30.9–14 and
Psalm 25.1–10; Colossians 1.1–14; Luke 10.25–37

AN UNEXPECTED HERO

Presentation
*Illustration: Pictures of worldly heroes from superhero cartoons,
popular culture and sport etc. What makes a hero? Do they live up
to expectations? Is their image really who they are? Read the story
of the good Samaritan. What makes a Christian hero? The Samaritan
was an unlikely candidate. His reputation worked against him. But
he showed love, unlike the priest or Levite. Unsung heroes just do
good quietly without an agent and attendant paparazzi!*

(277) Call to Worship

Psalm 25.1–2, 4–5 or Colossians 1.13–14

(278) Prayer of Adoration

God of vision, you have made a universe full of signs and symbols
Which can point our eyes to you.
You raised up prophets to guide your people, to warn the wanderers,
Because you are a God who cares and interacts and gets involved,
As you keep involving us in your wider story.
God of vision, we adore you.

God of vision, God of holiness, you are far above us.
We lift our hearts to worship you, and you rejoice to hear our praise.
In Jesus you came calling on us, living flesh in human form
Yet truly and fully God. Such mystery, Lord!
You are that mystery! You tickle our minds with questions and
    openings,
And you are the answer that speaks in our hearts.
God of vision, we adore you.

(279) Prayer of Confession

Wise God, we think of the idols we have made for ourselves; we
  may not call them idols,
but heroes or obsessions. Things we might turn to before we turn to
  you.
Silence
For putting things and people in your place:
We say sorry, and ask you to turn us around.
For not recognizing true heroines and heroes in our world:
We say sorry, and ask you to turn us around.
For stereotyping people and making them less or more than human:
We say sorry, and ask you to turn us around.
Silence
In your forgiving, Lord, you have turned us around to face you.
Now we can see the pain in your eyes and your heart that we have
  broken.
Now we can read and hear the words on your lips:
'Go in peace. Your sins are forgiven.'

(280) Prayer of Dedication

Everything we have comes from you, precious Father of hope;
You are our hero and our home;
Take what we have to offer, and make it acceptable through your
  grace.

(281) Prayer of Dismissal

Colossians 1.10–12

SUNDAY BETWEEN 17 AND 23 JULY INCLUSIVE

(Sixteenth Sunday in Ordinary Time)

Amos 8.1–12 and Psalm 52 or Genesis 18.1–10a and Psalm 15; Colossians 1.15–28; Luke 10.38–42

IMAGE OF THE INVISIBLE

Presentation

Illustration: Invisible writing: write a message in lemon juice and reveal it by heating it up with a candle (carefully!). What makes God visible to us in the world? Creation can show us part of his power. Jesus actually came to show us a glimpse of God himself, made flesh. The lemon juice writing was already there, as God is, but like the candle, Jesus lights and breathes warmth into our idea of God.

(282) Call to Worship

Psalm 52.9 or the following:

Come let us worship the invisible God:
Our eyes have not seen but our hearts sing praises.
Come let us tell of his wonderful works:
Our ears have not heard but our tongues tell his greatness.

(283) Prayer of Adoration

Invisible God, we adore you, unseen Creator of a visible universe!
You have been crafting and accomplishing forever,
Forming seas and lands, mountains and the mysteries of space out of nothing.
Before the first big bang of chemicals and particles
You have been planning for today and tomorrow.
Invisible God, we worship you.

Invisible God, we adore you, seen in Jesus, the Word made flesh.
You have been working among us since humankind first flourished,
Planning for our future and weaving your love around us.
The shadow of the cross was already swimming on the waters of creation,
And resurrection love was present at the first spark and tick of time.
Invisible God, we worship you.

Invisible God, we adore you, rushing like a winnowing wind over
the face of creation.
As Spirit we know you deep in our hearts, bubbling up to eternal life,
Unseen but real in our intellect, our emotions and our experience.
Invisible God, we worship you.

(284) Prayer of Confession

Unseen God, you see our secret thoughts and the things we are
hiding.
We are sorry for the things we think and do because we know we
can get away with it.
When nobody sees, we know we can cheat.
When nobody hears, we know we can gossip and lie.
Unseen God, forgive us.

(285) Prayer of Thanksgiving

For invisible things made visible:
We give you thanks and praise.
For the unseen wind we glimpse through waves and flowers dancing:
We give you thanks and praise.
For light that pierces hidden depths, revealing a wealth of marine
life:
We give you thanks and praise.
For Jesus who came to show us the heart of the unseen Father:
We give you thanks and praise.

(286) Meditation

*Read Luke's account of Martha and Mary. Play quiet music and
invite the congregation to picture first their tasks for the coming
week, and to invite the Lord to share these and keep us from 'busy-
ness' and stress. Secondly, invite them to spend a few minutes
dreaming and letting their imaginations take them on a journey, as
they picture themselves sitting at Jesus' feet. Fade the music out very
gently and allow time for silence before using the following:*

(287) Prayer of Dedication

Lord Jesus, we invite you into the world of our work:
We will share our tasks with you.
Lord Jesus, we invite you into our world of dreams:
We will dream our dreams in you.

(288) Prayer of Dismissal

May God make known to us now and in the days to come, the riches of the glories of his mystery, which is Christ in us, the hope of glory.

(289) Prayer of Dismissal

Let us go in the power and peace of Jesus Christ, the image of the invisible God, in the joy of the Holy Spirit.

SUNDAY BETWEEN 24 AND 30 JULY INCLUSIVE

(Seventeenth Sunday in Ordinary Time)

Hosea 1.2–10 and Psalm 85 or Genesis 18.20–32 and Psalm 138;
Colossians 2.6–15 (16–19); Luke 11.1–13

KNOCK, KNOCK

Presentation
Illustration: A mobile phone; get someone to keep interrupting what you are saying or reading by letting the phone ring. Let your exasperation grow a little as the interruptions persist! How do we react when someone keeps bothering us? Read Luke 11.1–13. We may pester family or friends to get us presents, but do we really get down to pestering God about important things?

(290) Call to Worship

Psalm 138.1–2 or Psalm 85.10–13

(291) Prayer of Adoration and Thanksgiving

God of love and faithfulness, we praise you.
We cannot keep track of you, energetic God, however we try,
Because you do not fit inside our narrow ideas.
You burst out in new ways, Creator of past, present and future.
We think we have you bottled and tamed in our words and pictures,
Then we find your Spirit is bounding and somersaulting out of our
    limits
And lapping the horizons with a rainbow of grace.
We will give you thanks with all our hearts.

(292) Prayer of Confession

Lord, your love endures forever, and you will not abandon us.
Knowing this, we are confident to pour out our hearts to you,
Confessing our failings and mix-ups.
So often we have forgotten to pray until we were in trouble.
We knock once then run away, afraid you will have forgotten us.
God of mercy, in your love for us, hear our prayer.
Silence

Forgive us when we have asked without believing we might receive.
Forgive us when we have prayed selfishly about others, wanting our will to be done.
Forgive us for hearing Jesus' teaching and letting it run like sand through our fingers.
God of mercy, in your love for us, hear our prayer.

(293) Prayer of Petition

Gracious God, give us the sticking power to work with you,
So that you can go on coaxing us into action,
Igniting us in prayer, transforming us into your likeness.
Generous Carer, give us the love that was in Jesus,
So that we may carry that love to the ones we meet,
Open ourselves to give and receive, and finally find rest in doing your will.

(294) Prayer of Dedication

Giving God, you would never give your children a scorpion for an egg,
A snake for a fish, or dynamite to play with.
You have given us every good thing.
You have given us Jesus and poured out your Holy Spirit
As the icing on our cake.
May we give with the same overflowing spirit of love and kindness,
All we have, all we are, and all we can be for Jesus' sake.

(295) Prayer of Dismissal

We have prayed together, sung with one voice, learned from one another the joy of unity;
Now let us go to live out the calling of our God in his world, bound together in Him.

SUNDAY BETWEEN 31 JULY AND 6 AUGUST INCLUSIVE

(Eighteenth Sunday in Ordinary Time)

Hosea 11.1–11 and Psalm 107.1–9, 43 or Ecclesiastes 1.2, 12–14;
2.18–23 and Psalm 49.1–12; Colossians 3.1–11; Luke 12.13–21

ALL IN ALL

Presentation

*Illustration: Large jar with coins inside. Illustrate the fable of the
monkey who tried to grab the money and could not withdraw its fist.
Greed can trap us. Read Luke 12.13–21. What use is money if you
are not free? How can we keep things in proportion? Which things
are most important in our lives? Paul tells us in Colossians 3. 11 that
Christ is 'all and in all'. Does this help us to set priorities and avoid
the trap of 'all kinds of greed'?*

(296) Call to Worship

Psalm 107.1–3 or 43

(297) Prayer of Adoration

Protecting God, saving your people, bringing them through
   treacherous places,
Watching and guiding, setting their feet on firm ground, we
   celebrate you.
In the face of our disobedience, you turn to your wandering ones,
Letting love triumph, for love is your name.
You are a great God, and greatly to be praised by your people.
How can we keep from worship when everything brings honour to
   you?
You will never give us up, for you have made us your children,
Made and moulded in your image and formed for your praise.

(298) Prayer of Confession

Christ is all and in all; his Spirit of truth is in us to help us to confess
the things we are ashamed to own up to, the things that break the
heart of our Lover and Lord.
Silence

121

We have been greedy and selfish:
We confess it and ask you to forgive.
We have been disobedient and sly:
We confess it and ask you to forgive.
We have been careless and misguided:
We confess it and ask you to forgive.
We have been cruel and graceless:
We confess it and ask you to forgive.
Silence
Christ is all and in all: we hear his words that turn our destructive
ways to ways of love.
Be at peace now; receive forgiveness and healing for all that sin
has tried to destroy.
**Christ is all and in all: we thank you and ask your help to keep
from falling into the same traps again.**

(299) Prayer of Petition

Read Colossians 3.1–4

Grant us, Lord, the vision to seek the things above, and to set our
    minds
On those things that come from you.
While our life is hidden with God, may we live on earth
As people who are sensitive to those who have not yet found a
    home in you.
Grant us the patience to watch for the revelation of Christ's glory.
May we never rest till our lives reveal that glory to all.

(300) Prayer of Dedication

Take these gifts into your hands, and use them in creative ways to
do your work in the world.
**Take us now into your hands, that we may be used to do that
work with you.**

(301) Prayer of Dismissal

Go to be rich towards your Maker, caught up in the mission of Christ,
enabled and filled with the colour and creativity of the Holy Spirit.

SUNDAY BETWEEN 7 AND 13 AUGUST INCLUSIVE

(Nineteenth Sunday in Ordinary Time)

Isaiah 1.1, 10–20 and Psalm 50.1–8,22–23 or Genesis 15.1–6 and Psalm 33.12–22; Hebrews 11.1–3, 8–16; Luke 12.32–40

WAITING FOR THE MASTER

Presentation
Illustration: Alarms; smoke alarms, burglar alarms, car alarms, screech alarms. Talk about how we need to do regular checks on the batteries and reliability of the alarms. Even when they are not actually going off to announce danger, they need to be 'on alert' or they will be useless when the moment comes! We tend to forget about smoke alarms most of the time, yet they are guarding us. In Luke, Jesus talks about being alert and ready for action. How can we do this? Would we feel ready if Jesus walked into church today?

(302) Call to Worship

Psalm 50.1–2 or Psalm 33.20–22

(303) Prayer of Adoration

God of waiting and wonder, we raise our hearts in worship to you.
From sunrise to the moment of the golden sunset,
When the night's stillness and hush bring peace after restless
    daylight hours,
Every moment of every day, you are watching over us:
Wonderful God we bring you our love and praise.

God of the universe, Lord of time and space,
You come to us with a human face of love.
Jesus our everything, who died for us and lives again in glory,
Has broken down barriers to stand where we stand,
To transform our lives by the Holy Spirit's power:
Wonderful God we bring you our love and praise.

(304) Prayer of Confession

'Do not be afraid, little flock.'
So you said to us, Lord Jesus, to encourage us and give us
  confidence.
We sometimes lose heart when our numbers are low.
Sometimes even in a crowd we get swept away by fears and doubts.
The truth is, alone or in a large company, we forget to listen to you.
We look at ourselves and those around us, and let ourselves get
  weighed down
Instead of lifting one another up.
We confess that we are often caught unready by what life brings.
We rush in suddenly, panicking, because we realize it is a long time
Since we listened to you, and walked with you for the joy of your
  company.
Forgive us and bring us your peace.
Do not be afraid, little flock. Your sins are forgiven.
Your Father is pleased to give you the Kingdom.

(305) Prayer of Petition

When prayer is needed: **make us ready.**
When compassion is needed: **make us ready.**
When action for justice is needed: **make us ready.**
When someone is in trouble: **make us ready.**
Your Kingdom is coming: **make us ready.**

(306) Prayer of Dedication

Gracious Friend, take us now, prepare us to live in readiness,
To live today equipped for your tomorrow.
Take our gifts and talents, and help us to live by that faith
Which is the assurance of things hoped for and the conviction of
  things not seen.

(307) Prayer of Dismissal

Go out into the world, ready to bring the Creator's love, ready to
share the good news of Jesus and ready always to respond with the
vision and wisdom of the Holy Spirit.

SUNDAY BETWEEN 14 AND 20 AUGUST INCLUSIVE

(Twentieth Sunday in Ordinary Time)

Isaiah 5.1–7 and Psalm 80.1–2, 8–19 or Jeremiah 23.23–29 and
Psalm 82; Hebrews 11.29–12.2; Luke 12.49–56

A CLOUD OF WITNESSES

Presentation
*Illustration: Perform a simple, obvious action in front of all the
church (this could be a comic mock 'robbery' from someone in the
front row, primed before the service etc.). Ask for witnesses.
Everyone has seen. What we have witnessed often (though not
always!) unites us. As Christians, now and in the past, we are all
witnesses of what Jesus has done. We are all part of a supportive
group. How do we show this? How do we let others join in? Those
who have been on the journey before us can still influence our
witness today.*

(308) Call to Worship

Psalm 80.1–2

(309) Prayer of Adoration

Mighty God, you have been active in every generation,
Stirring up your people to action and service,
Witnessing to what love is doing in the world.
Many have walked the extra mile into danger and difficulty,
Persecution and death.
God, you first loved us with a love that looks through death,
In Jesus you come healing wounds and tearing apart complacency,
Demanding choices and reordering the world in justice.
Mighty God, active in your world, we worship you.

(310) Prayer of Confession

God of time, you have surrounded us with a cloud of witnesses,
Those in every age who have died for love of you.
Forgive us for our own cowardice in the face of ridicule or rejection.

Forgive us for our complacency and love of maintaining the status quo.
Forgive us when our own witness to you becomes meaningless and sugar-coated.
You came to bring a peace that can divide and challenge:
Forgive us when we avoid hard choices and sit on the fence with a cushion!
Forgive us, Lord, and give us the courage to live and die for you.

(311) Prayer of Thanksgiving

For those who in the past cared little enough about their own safety
To walk out on a tricky tightrope for the gospel of God:
we give you thanks.
For those who in every age have risked their own comfort
To bring comfort to others:
we give you thanks.
For those who inspire us to try a little harder, walk a little further,
Risk a little more for the sake of Jesus:
we give you thanks.
For those who are tortured, mocked and flogged,
Imprisoned and separated from their loved ones:
we give you thanks.
For those who are rejected by their own families
For choosing to be part of the Christian family:
we give you thanks.
For giving us the chance to read your signs and live by your promises:
we give you thanks.

(312) Prayer of Dismissal

Creator who upholds us,
Go with us to dare for you.
Jesus who died for us,
Go with us to live and die with you.
Spirit who strengthens us,
Go with us to risk and run with you.

SUNDAY BETWEEN 21 AND 27 AUGUST INCLUSIVE

(Twenty-first Sunday in Ordinary Time)

Jeremiah 1.4–10 and Psalm 71.1–6 or Isaiah 58.9b–14 and Psalm 103.1–8; Hebrews 12.18–29; Luke 13.10–17

THE UNSHAKEABLE KINGDOM

Presentation

Illustration: Two large hoops placed with an overlap (like a giant Venn diagram). Tell the congregation that one hoop is the Kingdom of heaven and the other the kingdom of earth, and that we are going to sort items out according to where they belong. Sort cards marked 'healing', 'people', 'prophet', 'Jesus' etc. into the hoops. It will quickly emerge that for many things, there is no such dividing line. Read Hebrews 12.18–29. What does this tell us about heaven and earth? In Luke, Jesus healed on the Sabbath, breaking down dividing lines between heavenly and earthly things in our minds. Push the two hoops together.

(313) Call to Worship

Psalm 103.1–2 or Psalm 71.5–6

(314) Prayer of Adoration

Creator God, your Kingdom can never be shaken,
You are beyond our touch yet as close as our dearest friend.
Bless the Lord: **May all that is in us bless his holy name!**
God without limits, you hold everything in your hands,
To pluck up and pull down, to destroy and overthrow,
To build and plant, to benefit and bless.
Bless the Lord: **May all that is in us bless his holy name!**
God you love and listen, we call to you and you answer us in time
    of need.
Though your power can shake kingdoms and remove created things,
Yet in your rainbow promise you tell us that you will not destroy us.
We adore you and celebrate with awe the love that saves us in Jesus.
Bless the Lord: **May all that is in us bless his holy name!**

(315) Prayer of Thanksgiving

Read Luke 13.10–17

Thank you, Jesus, for your healing power,
Straightening us out when we are bent over with pain or worries:
Thank you, loving God, bringing healing to your people.
Thank you, Jesus, for your healing power,
Straightening us out when we get the wrong ideas about you and
    your Kingdom:
Thank you, loving God, bringing healing to your people.
Thank you, Jesus, for your healing power,
Straightening out your church when it puts traditions above God's
    groundbreaking love:
Thank you, loving God, bringing healing to your people.

(316) Prayer of Confession

God, you have known us before you formed us inside the womb.
We can hide nothing from you. You know us inside out.
We confess all the wrong things we try to keep from others and
    from you.
Inside our clutching fists we hide the good things we could we
    sharing.
Behind our tight lips we bite back the kind words we could be
    saying.
Inside our hidden heart we keep the love and generous help we
    could be giving.
Locked in our judgmental minds we keep the prejudice and spite
    you could be healing.
Forgive us, Giver of Love: open us up and shake out from all the
    hidden places the things that bind and damage.
Silence
With most tender hands you shake us up, soothe our pain, and
    forgive our sin.
Thank you, forgiving Healer.

(317) Prayer of Dedication

**Take us and our gifts, though we feel small, and do big things
with them and us!**

(318) Prayer of Dismissal

Go with God, to make mistakes and learn from them, to make friends and share his love with them and to make a difference wherever he may send you.

SUNDAY BETWEEN 28 AUGUST AND 3 SEPTEMBER INCLUSIVE

(Twenty-second Sunday in Ordinary Time)

Jeremiah 2.4–13 and Psalm 81.1, 10–16 or Ecclesiasticus 10.12–18 or Proverbs 25.6–7 and Psalm 112; Hebrews 13.1–8, 15–16; Luke 14.1, 7–14

PARTY FOR THE POOR

Presentation
Illustration: Party invitations, party bags etc. Talk about the way giving party bags and returning invitations can get out of hand sometimes. (Anyone with young children will know this!) Just inviting friends can soon escalate into a large number. Does it end up as trying to 'keep up' with expectations? Does what you are celebrating get lost? In Luke, Jesus talks about inviting those who really need a party. These ones might not be able to give a 'party bag' of goodies back. The 'party bag' at Jesus' banquet comes from God.

(319) Call to Worship

Psalm 81.1 or the following:

The Lord is our helper: **We will not be afraid!**
Who will join us to celebrate our God?
Throw open the doors so everyone may come in!

(320) Prayer of Adoration

Lord of our lives, God of our world, we gather to celebrate you.
You rule the universe, its heights and depths,
From the top of the mountain to the ocean floor,
From the furthest planet to the hairs on our head.
Lord of our lives, God of our world, we gather to worship you.

You are in the dripping of the rain and the drumming of beats and
    bar-lines,
Everything has its music and sings your praise!
We come to a cosmic party, a universal celebration of our Creator!
Guest of honour, you put us in our place,

And ask us to throw our doors wide open to whoever wants to join
in!
Lord of our lives, God of our world, we gather to worship you.

(321) Prayer of Thanksgiving

Lord, thank you for tipping us upside down to see things better!
Thank you for putting the humble in a place of honour
And pulling the chair out from under the arrogant.
Thank you for taking us back to yourself when we run away,
Too proud to realize we need you.
Thank you for making nonsense of our worldly ways,
When we prefer to stick with the people who make us feel important.
Thank you for leading us to party with the powerless,
To learn we are all special when the party is in your honour!

(322) Prayer of Petition

Read Hebrews 13.1–8

Lord, give us the mutual love that binds us together,
But let us never become a clique that keeps people away from you.
Give us the hospitality to make a welcome for strangers
And then may they become friends, bound in that mutual love.
Give us the grace to entertain unsuspected angels
And the grace to share all we have for your sake.

(323) Prayer of Dedication

What we give, may we give with joy:
Accept it, Lord, as you accept us.
The new friends we make, may we treat with respect:
Accept them, Lord, as you accept us.
What we dream from today, may we dream with you:
Accept us, Lord, for Jesus' sake.

(324) Prayer of Dismissal

The circle of God's love, like ripples in the water, is widening and
welcoming:
We go, to widen our circle of love so nobody stands outside.

SUNDAY BETWEEN 4 AND 10 SEPTEMBER INCLUSIVE

(Twenty-third Sunday in Ordinary Time)

Jeremiah 18.1–11 and Psalm 139.1–6, 13–18 or
Deuteronomy 30.15–20 and Psalm 1; Philemon 1–21; Luke 14.25–33

COUNTING THE COST

Presentation
Illustration: Builder's plans of church or house, or start to build something with too few bricks to complete it. Which things are needed in planning a new venture? Things we need to consider include costs, preparing the site, planning permission (and the time this takes!) Have old buildings had to be pulled down to make way for new in our area? Image of the potter reshaping old and making new, at cost and risk. Jesus' words in Luke warn us to be aware of the costs involved in the venture of following him. Which things might we need to consider?

(325) Call to Worship
Psalm 139.17–18

(326) Prayer of Adoration

God of the heavens and the earth,
There is nothing in all creation that is beyond your power
For you have made everything that is, seen and unseen.
Father God, we adore you!

You are the one who shapes and reshapes,
Bringing greater blessings and more astonishing depths of wonder
Than we can know or name.
Father God, we adore you!

You are the Potter, fashioning what is fragile with tender hands
Or shattering what is evil, making all things new.
Father God, we adore you!

(327) Prayer of Confession

Lord, we have not counted the cost of following you.
We have thought we could come with our sins unforgiven,
With our eyes on our possessions, with our lives unchanged.
Forgive us, Lord, and reshape us in your image.

Lord, we have not made estimates beyond the foundations.
We have thought we could reach heaven
While we left our burdens on the poor and the powerless.
Forgive us, Lord, and reshape us in your image.

Lord, we have not packed enough for the journey.
We thought we could get by without the food of your word,
Without your spirit to empower, without the map of your guidance.
Forgive us, Lord, and reshape us in your image.

(328) Prayer of Petition

Lord, we want to be able to carry the cross and follow you:
Give us firmness of purpose when we dither and shuffle our feet.
Give us vision and wisdom when we start digging on the wrong
site.
Give us humility and patience to be as well as do.
Give us joy and resilience to set out knowing we can arrive.
Give us the refreshment of the Holy Spirit, to complete the work
begun with you.
Give us all these things, Lord, and what we cannot ask, through
ignorance or fear,
Make known to us and place within the orbit of our adventure.

(329) Prayer of Dismissal

Let us go adventuring with God, counting the cost and still setting
out, knowing our weaknesses and trusting him for our strength,
knowing his love for us, and rejoicing in him forever.

SUNDAY BETWEEN 11 AND 17 SEPTEMBER INCLUSIVE

(Twenty-fourth Sunday in Ordinary Time)

Jeremiah 4.11–12, 22–28 and Psalm 14 or Exodus 32.7–14 and
Psalm 51.1–10; I Timothy 1.12–17; Luke 15.1–10

LOST AND FOUND

Presentation

*Illustration: Show items that could turn up in a lost and found
department, i.e. umbrellas, glasses, false teeth! How do we feel to get
something back that is lost? Sometimes if it is unimportant, we do not
even notice it is gone. Some things people are too embarrassed
about, and disown (hence some of the extraordinary things people
never reclaim!) Compare the joy in the stories of Jesus about the
recovery of the coin and the lost sheep. We do not embarrass God,
nor are we unimportant to him. He rejoices to bring us home!*

(330) Call to Worship

Come into God's house with gladness!
We come to worship him with shouts of joy!
When we were lost he came to find us.
We run to his arms where we find our home!

(331) Prayer of Adoration

God of mercy and miracle, your love coaxes creation out of nothing;
Your holy Word speaks order out of seething atoms in time and
    space.
Nothing is too difficult for you and you are in everything that is.
We search for words to name you, and find you have named
    yourself
In the subtle colours of sunrise and the vast sweep of the oceans.
You have told your story in flesh and blood, in Jesus,
Gathering in your lost people from the furthest reaches of their
    wandering.
God of mercy and miracle, we name you Lord of all.

God of mercy and miracle, when your people wander
You come looking for them in forgotten corners and desert places.
On the green hills of hope you come as Shepherd to gather your
  lost sheep
And bring them home.
They know your voice, and recognize your calling.
Anger and hurt dissolve back into mercy,
Reflecting your name and nature, which is Love.
God of mercy and miracle, we name you Lord of all.

(332) Prayer of Confession

Lord, we are truly sorry for all the golden calves we have made
To worship instead of you.
We have poured our energies and devotion out on things that
  wither or rust.
We are truly sorry: we reach out and receive your forgiveness.
Lord, we are truly sorry that we have so often gone off on detours,
Wandering through your landscape.
We have acted like strangers and strays in your fold of love.
We are truly sorry: we reach out and receive your forgiveness.

(333) Meditation

Crouched by this rock, sheltered from sight, no one will find me.
Here all alone, I've escaped from the probing crook, the staff and
  the eye that guides me.
No one will find me. I wish someone would.
Silence
I know the voice. I recognize the step. Suddenly we are both running.
My Shepherd, my Master. Please take me home with you.

(334) Prayer of Dedication

Scattered gifts you gather, Lord; **take what we can give.**
Scattered coins you seek, Lord; **take and use what is yours.**
Scattered sheep you find, Lord; **gather us into your heart.**

(335) Prayer of Dismissal

I Timothy 1.17

SUNDAY BETWEEN 18 AND 24 SEPTEMBER INCLUSIVE

(Twenty-fifth Sunday in Ordinary Time)

Jeremiah 8.18–9.1 and Psalm 79.1–9 or Amos 8.4–7 and Psalm 113;
I Timothy 2.1–7; Luke 16.1–13

TWO MASTERS

Presentation
*Illustration: Two 'masters' read out two sets of contrary instructions
to a third party, e.g. the first says 'Turn right' and 'Behind you!'
while the second is urging 'Turn left' and 'Go forward!' How does
this work out? Did the one following orders obey the one closest, or
loudest, or were they simply paralysed by indecision? Following two
masters, we have to disappoint, ignore, disobey or compromise!
Read Luke 16.13. If we follow God as our priority can we sort our
priorities out more clearly when difficult choices come?*

(336) Call to Worship

Psalm 113.1–3 or 4–5

(337) Prayer of Adoration

From the rising of the sun to the place where it sets
The Lord's name is to be praised.
Dear Lord our God, how excellent is your name in all the earth!
Your name is Love; your name is 'I am',
Present from the beginning to the time yet to be revealed.
From the rising of the sun to the place where it sets:
The Lord's name is to be praised.

You have made the earth teem with an amazing variety of life.
You have made harvests to share, holidays to refresh us,
Laughter to bring us together, animals to care for and bring out the
    best in us.
You given us families and friends, music and silence, and a place
    in your creation.
From the rising of the sun to the place where it sets:
The Lord's name is to be praised.

(338) Prayer of Thanksgiving

We thank you for setting us in a world
That challenges us to grow.
We thank you that you bring us down to earth when we have our
head in the clouds.
We thank you for generosity that conquers greed, for love that
soothes away fear and for eternity that puts temporary things into
perspective.
We thank you that when our life on earth is over, we have a place
in heaven with you.

(339) Prayer of Confession

Compassionate God, we ask your forgiveness:
for the times we are foolish and worldly;
for the times we forget who is the one we should follow;
for the times we trample on the needy and strangle hope in the poor;
for the times we take more than we can give;
for the times we speak and dominate more than we listen and
empathize.
Silence
We receive the healing that frees us to live in your love.

(340) Prayer of Dedication

May these gifts be used to bring hope to the hopeless.
Take us, Lord, and make us faithful in the little things, so that in
the fullness of time,
You will be able to entrust us with all you have planned.
Take all we have, Lord, and make us a fragrant sacrifice of love.

(341) Prayer of Dismissal

Go to work with God in the world, to deal wisely with the shrewd, to
be at one with the humble, to know the one you are serving and to
bring glory to his name.

SUNDAY BETWEEN 25 SEPTEMBER AND 1 OCTOBER INCLUSIVE

(Twenty-sixth Sunday in Ordinary Time)

Jeremiah 32.1–3a, 6–15 and Psalm 91.1–6, 14–16 or Amos 6.1a, 4–7 and Psalm 146; I Timothy 6.6–19; Luke 16.19–31

LIFE THAT REALLY IS LIFE

Presentation
Illustration: Evidence. Videos, cassettes, written evidence, CD Roms; which are we more likely to believe? Is some evidence more reliable than another kind? Do we usually believe what suits us best? If someone says something we want to hear, we may well agree, whatever the evidence! Talk about the story of Lazarus and the rich man who had not been convinced by anything before death came. Why? Because he was quite content to be rich! Now read I Timothy 6.19. What convinces us that with God we will have 'life that really is life'?

(342) Call to Worship

Psalm 91.1–2 or Psalm 146.1–6

(343) Prayer of Adoration

We will praise the Lord as long as life lasts!
We will sing praises to our God as long as we are alive!
Happy are those who have their hope in the Lord!
He made the heavens and seas.
He made everything that is in them.
The Lord keeps his promise forever.
He sets the prisoners free: **Alleluia!**
He opens the eyes of the blind: **Praise the Lord!**
He lifts up those who are bowed down: **Alleluia!**
He loves the righteous and cares for the stranger: **Praise the Lord!**
He looks after the widow and the orphan: **Alleluia!**
He frustrates the plans of wicked people: **Praise the Lord!**
The Lord shall reign forever!

(344) Prayer of Confession

Read I Timothy 6.6–19

Lord, through Paul you taught us that we should be content with
what we have.
We confess to you that we are often restless for more than we need.
We are sorry for being gripped by temptation through wanting
more and more.
We run around, trapped by senseless and harmful desires.
We chase the butterflies of fame, popularity, wit and wealth.
Forgive us, Lord.
Silence
In the silence, we hear your word of peace that heals us and sets us
back on our feet.

(345) Prayer of Thanksgiving

Thank you, Lord, for giving us the kind of wealth the world cannot
give us:
For giving us Jesus, our best Friend and our Saviour,
For giving us the Holy Spirit, who makes his home in our hearts,
For giving us eternal life, where one day we will live with you.

(346) Prayer of Petition

Give us the wisdom to believe the evidence that counts.
Help us to know whom to trust, and to be trustworthy ourselves.
Teach us to seek you in every situation,
So we can learn to recognize you in those we often scorn.
Give us your Spirit's clear wise leading,
So we may lay hold on that which really is life.

(347) Prayer of Dismissal

Let us go together in the joyful hope of eternal life and in the
brightness of the promise that God is with us this day and forever
more.

SUNDAY BETWEEN 2 AND 8 OCTOBER INCLUSIVE

(Twenty-seventh Sunday in Ordinary Time)

Lamentations 1.1–6 and Lamentations 3.19–26 or Psalm 137 or
Habakkuk 1.1–4; 2.1–4 and Psalm 37.1–9; II Timothy 1.1–14;
Luke 17.5–10

A SEED OF FAITH

Presentation
*Illustration: A seed and its plant (mustard if available). Compare
size of seed and plant. Can we tell from how something begins how
big it will be? What does the seed need to grow into a plant? It is not
enough just to 'practise' faith, though this is a start. We need God to
water our faith to help it grow stronger. Genetic modifications apart,
seeds grow into the plants they are designed to be. God can take the
tiniest things and help them grow into what they were intended to be
in him.*

(348) Call to Worship

Psalm 37.4–6 or Lamentation 3.22–24

(349) Prayer of Adoration

Eternal God, you are everything to your children:
You entrust your good treasures to us in your Son Jesus Christ and
    bring us alive with the tingle and touch of your creative Spirit.
Pole to pole, the heavens trace intricate patterns of incandescence
    that you have drawn.
Shore to shore, the oceans roar and frost the shingle with lace of
    salt and foam.
The tantrums of the hurricane and the hanging silence of the
    mountains tell out your beauty, your sense of humour and your
    majesty.
We adore you, Lord God, for everything you are to us.

(350) Prayer of Confession

Let us ask together for the Holy Spirit to show us our faults, help
    us to confess them,

And bring us into God's forgiving grace.
Silence
We are sorry, Lord, for grieving and worrying you in what we have
   done in these past days.
Forgive us for our lack of faith and lack of eagerness to increase it.
Forgive us for our lack of vision as we stare down at our shoes.
Forgive us for our lack of prayer, sending up arrows only in times
   of need.
Forgive us for our lack of love, and warm our hearts with the fire
   of your devotion.
Silence
We leave our burdens of sin with God and go on together with a
   lighter step.

(351) Prayer of Thanksgiving

For the friends who sit around us: **Thank you, Lord.**
For the friends who are far away from us: **Thank you, Lord.**
For the friends who make us sit up and think about you: **Thank
   you, Lord.**
For the friends who help increase our faith: **Thank you, Lord.**
For the friends whom we have yet to meet: **Thank you, Lord.**
For the friends who have gone to be with you: **Thank you, Lord.**

(352) Prayer of Dedication

The steadfast love of the Lord never fails us:
His mercies to us never come to an end.
They are new every morning:
Great is your faithfulness!
In the light of your unending faithfulness and mercy,
We turn to you with our gifts, asking you to make them seeds of
   something bigger.
We turn to you with our whole lives, asking you to make us more
   faithful day by day.

(353) Prayer of Dismissal

May the Lord write his name on our hearts, so plain that a runner
   may read it;
May the Lord plant a seed of faith in us and water it with his Spirit;
May the Lord place his love in us and walk with us as we take it to
   the waiting world.

SUNDAY BETWEEN 9 AND 15 OCTOBER INCLUSIVE

(Twenty-eighth Sunday in Ordinary Time)

Jeremiah 29.1, 4–7 and Psalm 66.1–12 or II Kings 5.1–3, 7–15c and Psalm 111; II Timothy 2.8–15; Luke 17.11–19

THANK YOU, JESUS

Presentation

Illustration: A thank you letter. Do we always write ours after birthdays and Christmas? Why say thank you? It's all about love and preserving a relationship with give and take. The Samaritan with the skin problem returned as a living thank you letter to Jesus. His relationship with God could grow through his decision to say thank you in return for his healing. He met Jesus again, face to face. The others missed this chance to deepen a relationship with God. How do we say thank you to Jesus?

(354) Call to Worship

Psalm 66.1–4, 8–12 or Psalm 111.10

(355) Prayer of Adoration and Thanksgiving

Living God, we have come into your house
To worship and adore you, in silence and singing, penitence and
  prayer.
Your Word cannot be chained or contained in a straitjacket of
  formality.
Your life comes leaping, radiant with promises,
Pouring into our world, recreating us for love.
Let us bless our God together:
Make the voice of his praise be heard.

Living Christ, we come to give thanks to you,
For moving among us with ears tuned to hear our deepest needs
And hands stretched out to bless and heal us.
We praise and thank you for the wonder of knowing you,
As you teach and shock and challenge us, calling us to follow you.
Let us bless our God together:
Make the voice of his praise be heard.

Living Spirit, we come to worship you and thank you
For breathing through our world the beauty of God's presence,
Peeling back the dull film of our understanding
To reveal in true colours the truth of God.
Let us bless our God together:
Make the voice of his praise be heard.

(356) Prayer of Confession

Lord, like the ten lepers, we have often forgotten to thank you
For your great gifts to us. We have hurried away, on our daily
    business,
Putting you to the back of our minds until it was more convenient.
Forgive us when we make you a Sunday God, our Lord of special
    occasions.
Forgive us when we forget you are the very fabric from which our
    lives are woven:
Hear us, Lord, and forgive us in your mercy.

Lord, forgive us for all the times we have denied you,
Or shrunk from showing that we are your disciples.
Forgive us for wrangling over words and splitting hairs
Especially when this has held people back from your Kingdom.
Forgive us for our faithlessness; Lord, you remain faithful,
For you cannot deny your very nature.
On this we depend and turn afresh to you:
Hear us, Lord, and forgive us in your mercy.

(357) Prayer of Dismissal

Go in the blessing of the Creator:
We go to live to the Creator's glory.
Go in the blessing of Christ:
We go to follow in Christ's footsteps.
Go in the blessing of the Holy Spirit:
We go to act in the Spirit's power.
We are blessed on our way: **we are blessed indeed!**

SUNDAY BETWEEN 16 AND 22 OCTOBER INCLUSIVE

(Twenty-ninth Sunday in Ordinary Time)

Jeremiah 31.27–34 and Psalm 119.97–104 or Genesis 32.22–31 and Psalm 121; II Timothy 3.14–4.5; Luke 18.1–8

EQUIPPED FOR EVERY GOOD WORK

Presentation
Illustration: Equipment for a specific job (this will vary according to what the congregation or leader have to offer). Draw out how the equipment helps with the job. Can it be used in other less obvious ways? Show a variety of Bible versions. We all have favourite Bibles, or treasured passages. Share some of these. The Bible can speak to us all in personal and unique ways. It can be useful in different times of need. List some of these. Read I Timothy 3.14–16. Are there ways that scripture should not be used?

(358) Call to Worship

Psalm 121.1–4

(359) Prayer of Adoration

Lord God, Maker of heaven and earth, we lift our eyes to the hills,
But where is the source of our help?
Our help comes from the Lord and we worship him.
Lord, you are always watching over your world,
Delighting to see your children worshipping freely.
You watch over our going out and our return,
Concerned with our laughter and tears, our successes and our
    suffering.
Where is the source of our help?
Our help comes from the Lord and we worship him.
Lord, your words are sweet to our taste,
Sweeter than honey to our mouths.
You teach us this and every day to trust in you
And depend on Jesus, who makes us one.
Where is the source of our help?
Our help comes from the Lord and we worship him.

(360) Prayer of Confession

Read Genesis 32.22–31

Wrestling God, we confess that we often struggle against you.
When we struggle against you to get our own way:
Forgive us and heal us.
When we wrestle with you and then run off to sulk:
Forgive us and heal us.
When we fight against others with cruel words and sarcasm:
Forgive us and heal us.
Lord, we carry the wounds of our struggles like a hip out of joint.
We do not want to let you go unless you bless us.
Bless us with your healing forgiveness.

(361) Prayer of Thanksgiving

Read II Timothy 3.14–4.5

Thank you, living Word, for your Holy Scripture,
Inspired by God and useful for teaching:
For opportunities for us to hear your word as children and young
    people
From junior church and youth fellowships, from clubs and
    uniformed organizations,
For scriptures that put our lives under the spotlight and ask hard
    questions,
For the light the Holy Spirit throws on the words we read,
For equipping us for every good work.

(362) Prayer of Dedication

Lord God, you have given us the gifts and resources
To equip us for every good work.
These gifts we now offer back into your strong, safe hands,
Knowing that you will take them and bless them.
Use them powerfully, Lord, in the building of your Kingdom.
Use us powerfully, Lord, in the building of your Kingdom.

(363) Prayer of Dismissal

Psalm 121.7–8

SUNDAY BETWEEN 23 AND 29 OCTOBER INCLUSIVE

(Thirtieth Sunday in Ordinary Time)

Joel 2.23–32 and Psalm 65 or Ecclesiasticus 35.12–17 or
Jeremiah 14.7–10, 19–22 and Psalm 84.1–7; II Timothy 4.6–8, 16–18;
Luke 18.9–14

BE HUMBLE

Presentation
Illustration: Peacocks and sparrows. Display pictures of plumage designed to attract attention alongside natural camouflage. How is this achieved in the animal kingdom? Loud calls, bright feathers etc. Some blend into background by drawing attention away from themselves. How and why do humans do this? Not always the brightest/loudest who is doing best! Jesus warns us to let God determine who is to be humbled or lifted up.

(364) Call to Worship

Psalm 84.1–4 or Psalm 65.1–4

(365) Prayer of Adoration

Creator God, receive our praise and may our worship make you glad.
You have fastened the roots of the mountains in place
And stilled the roaring of the seas.
Across the globe, all people tremble at your awesome signs;
You make the dawn and dusk sing.
You water the earth and prepare for the harvest,
Drenching furrows and smoothing out the ridges.
Creator God: **we bring you our praise and adoration.**
God of all glory, you crown the year with your goodness
And all your paths overflow with peace.
You make the fields of the wilderness rich for grazing
And the hills are clothed with joy.
In your wonderful world, even the meadows and valleys shout and
    sing for joy.
Creator God: **we bring you our praise and adoration.**

(366) Prayer of Confession

Lord, when we point to what we have done,
When we proclaim ourselves the monarch of our own castle:
Forgive us and quieten us with your humble love.
Lord, when we do good deeds for others to applaud:
Forgive us and quieten us with your humble love.
When we feel self-satisfied that we are not like our neighbour:
Forgive us and quieten us with your humble love.

(367) Prayer of Thanksgiving

Read II Timothy 4.6–8

Thank you, Righteous Judge, for those who have fought their fight
    for you,
Who have finished the race at your side and have kept the faith for
    Jesus' sake.
We thank you that you have promised a crown of righteousness
To all who have been yearning and aching for your appearance.
Thank you for the strength you give in hours of struggle
When others have abandoned us and left us for dead in the dark.
Thank you for making your message sing through the lips of your
    saints:
To God be the glory for ever.

(368) Prayer of Dedication

Lord, we give you these gifts,
Not so that we can blow our own trumpet or gain points with our
    goodness,
But so that you can use them for your glory,
And humble us to serve you as you deserve.

(369) Prayer of Dismissal

Go humbly with God, so that through your love for him, others may
worship him and give him all the glory.

ALL SAINTS (1 NOVEMBER)

Daniel 7.1–3, 15–18; Psalm 149; Ephesians 1.11–23; Luke 6.20–31

LET THE FAITHFUL REJOICE

Presentation

Illustration: Names. Arm yourself with a dictionary of the meaning of Christian names. (It will be helpful to prepare for some names you know will be present, including your own!) Draw out how special our names are to us, at baptism, spoken by a loved one, etc. Are we named after someone special in our family? God loves all his people and put Christ above 'every name that is named'. In the Old Testament, people sometimes had new names to reflect their life in God. Paul gave thanks for the Ephesians' love 'for all the saints'. We are here to celebrate individuals in every age, bound together in the love of Christ.

(370) Call to Worship

Psalm 149.1–5

(371) Prayer of Adoration

Sing to the Lord a new song!
We will sing his praise in the congregation of the faithful!
Lord, in every age you have been inspiring your people
To works of love and power in your name.
You are a God who delights in all your children,
Placing Christ as the head over all things for the church.
Past, present and future, your crowd of saints adore you and we
    join in chorus:
Sing to the Lord a new song!
We will sing his praise in the congregation of the faithful!
Lord, we celebrate Christ, the name above every name;
He has given strength to his people in their suffering
And has lifted them in him to glory.
May we be named among your faithful
And live to sing your praises in the cloud of witnesses:
Sing to the Lord a new song!
We will sing his praise in the congregation of the faithful!

(372) Prayer of Confession

As we sing and celebrate your faithful followers in every age,
We are conscious that we have trouble with individuals.
We are jealous of others' spiritual stature.
We are critical of those whose faith burns in a different way from
   ours.
We are cynical about the truth of ancient stories
That tell how saints have shown your immortal love.
**Forgive us, Lover of your people, and gather us at last into
   your glorious company**.

(373) Prayer of Thanksgiving

For those who dream dreams: **Most High, we thank you.**
For those who carry their cross: **Most High, we thank you.**
For those who risk all for the gospel: **Most High, we thank you.**
For those who build bridges: **Most High, we thank you.**
For those whom the world has forgotten: **Most High, we thank you.**
For those who point us to heaven: **Most High, we thank you.**

(374) Prayer of Dedication

Lord God, your holy ones will possess the Kingdom forever;
Receive our offering out of the riches that you have given to your
   children
At every season of created time. Accept what we bring, for Jesus'
   sake.

(375) Prayer of Dismissal

God of the faithful, go with us into your world, where you are
already working with those who love you.
Inspire us to great acts for you, humble us for daily service, and
bring us at the last to receive and possess the Kingdom forever, by
your grace and mercy.

SUNDAY BETWEEN 30 OCTOBER AND 5 NOVEMBER INCLUSIVE

(Thirty-first Sunday in Ordinary Time)

Habakkuk 1.1–4; 2.1–4 and Psalm 119.137–144 or Isaiah 1.10–18 and Psalm 32.1–7; II Thessalonians 1.1–4,11–12; Luke 19.1–10

COME ON DOWN!

Presentation

Illustration: Binoculars and a chair. Standing on the chair scanning the congregation with the binoculars, ask to what lengths we will go to get a good view. A rare bird or an important event may make us eager to get a grandstand view. Introduce Zacchaeus, getting up high in a tree to see Jesus. We need to prepare ourselves for an important encounter. Zacchaeus' height held him back, so he climbed, to overcome it. Jesus changed his life. How can we overcome what holds us back to see Jesus more clearly?

(376) Call to Worship

Psalm 119.137–138 or Psalm 32.6–7

(377) Prayer of Adoration

God of the great and the little in creation,
You have made everything to work together for good.
We worship you, climbing to high places to catch a glimpse of your
    face.
We often feel small and of little account,
For you are too great for our understanding to grasp.
Yet you care and provide for the tiniest and the least
And the weak and powerless are held in the palm of your hand.
From the littlest to the tallest,
From the height to the depth,
From the top to the bottom,
Always and everywhere
We give you our joyful praise!

(378) Prayer of Confession

Compassion made flesh for us, Lord of our life:
We say sorry for the times we have made others feel small.
Silence
Though our sins are like scarlet:
They shall be like snow.
We say sorry for letting the way we were made hold us back.
Silence
Though our sins are like scarlet:
They shall be like snow.
We say sorry for the times we made no effort to see you, Lord.
Silence
Though our sins are like scarlet:
They shall be like snow.

(379) Prayer of Thanksgiving

Thank you for the little things that delight us:
For people who do not make a big splash about serving you,
But do it just the same.
Thank you for caring about the ones the world ignores.
You never look or speak over our heads, but right into our hearts.

(380) Prayer of Petition

Give us eyes to see you when a crowd of things gets in the way.
Lift us up to meet you when we feel tied to the ground by daily tasks.
Call us down from our high horse whenever we get on it.
Come into our homes to be with us, bringing your salvation.

(381) Prayer of Dismissal

Based on II Thessalonians 1.12

May the name of our Lord Jesus be glorified in us and we in him, according to the grace of our God and the Lord Jesus Christ.

SUNDAY BETWEEN 6 AND 12 NOVEMBER INCLUSIVE

(Thirty-second Sunday in Ordinary Time)

Haggai 1.15b – 2.9 and Psalm 145.1–5, 17–21 (or Psalm 98) or
Job 19.23–27a and Psalm 17.1–9; II Thessalonians 2.1–5, 13–17;
Luke 20.27–38

GOD OF THE LIVING

Presentation

Illustration: A time-line, drawn on a length of paper: if possible use points in the history of the local congregation. Place various events and people along the line. Where do we fit in? Where is God? Draw out how we sometimes see history in a linear way. Yet God is never past, present or future only. He is part of our experience in every age. He brings our experience of life into the context of the whole world and of all time. Read the Gospel passage in light of what you have discovered together.

(382) Call to Worship

Psalm 17.6–9, Psalm 145.1–4 or Psalm 98.1–3

(383) Prayer of Adoration

Sing to the Lord a new song:
For he has done marvellous things.
Every day we will bless our God:
And praise his name forever and ever.
Let the seas sing and the river clap hands
For God is our righteous Judge and our joy.
God of the living, your life is everywhere: in the energies of creation,
In the crafts and celebrations of humankind,
In plants and animals vibrant and unique,
In complicated chemistry that holds your world together.
Sing to the Lord a new song:
For he has done marvellous things.

(384) Prayer of Confession

Hear our cry, Lord, in your mercy.
You listen to our prayer and you forgive us.

When we have acted as if you were far away,
Consigning you to history so we could suit ourselves today:
Hear our cry, Lord, in your mercy.
You listen to our prayer and you forgive us.

When we have been so wrapped up in our own needs
That we have lost sight of the needs of those around us:
Hear our cry, Lord, in your mercy.
You listen to our prayer and you forgive us.

(385) Prayer of Petition

Give us what we need, in your Spirit, to live our lives by faith:
Your vision, when we are blindfolded by self-interest.
Your patience, when we burning on the short fuse of our own temper.
Your peace, when we are punch-drunk from the jabbing fist of
    commitments.
Your music, when our nerves are frazzled by the discord of many
    demands.
Your promise, when we feel too let down to trust ourselves again.
Your eternity, to give us hope in the rush of today.

(386) Prayer of Dedication

God of goodness:
May we live our lives to bring good things to others.
God of justice:
May we live our lives to bring your justice to others.
God of change:
May we live our lives always willing to be changed.
God of growth:
May we live our lives always willing to grow in you.
God of sharing, our gifts we place in your hands:
May we share what we have to be used for the sake of your love.

(389) Prayer of Dismissal

II Thessalonians 2.16–17

SUNDAY BETWEEN 13 AND 19 NOVEMBER INCLUSIVE

(Thirty-third Sunday in Ordinary Time)

Isaiah 65.17–25 and Isaiah 12 or Malachi 4.1–2a and Psalm 98;
II Thessalonians 3.6–13; Luke 21.5–19

DON'T BE LED ASTRAY!

Presentation

Illustration: Tuning fork or pitch pipes. Try to involve the organist or music makers in explaining how to pitch a note. Experiment with 'wrong' notes, and let the tuning fork lead you back to the true pitch. Everyone can join in by humming the notes chosen and hearing the difference between right and wrong notes. Jesus warns us not to be led astray by false voices. Listening to his 'perfect pitch' can help keep us in tune with him when other influences come. How do we listen for him?

(388) Call to Worship

Isaiah 65.17–19, Isaiah 12.2–3 or 4–6, or Psalm 98.1–3

(389) Prayer of Adoration

God of energy, joy and silence,
Everywhere your creation is waking to bring you praise.
We come as your own to be part of your story,
We come as your children to be gathered and blessed.
We are here because we love you:
We come to adore you, Love of our life!
God who creates, God who cares for all,
We want to be part of the new things you are doing.
Your promise holds up the heavens,
Your salvation saves your people.
We are here because we love you:
We come to adore you, Love of our life!

(390) Prayer of Confession

We turn again to you, loving Lord God:
Forgive and change us.
We have got it wrong again:
In things done and things said.
We have got it wrong again:
In things planned and things wasted.
We have broken your heart again:
With best intentions and lazy hearts.
We have broken your heart again:
In shunning enemies and hurting friends.
We turn again to you, loving Lord God:
Forgive and change us.

(391) Prayer of Thanksgiving

For doing new things, and giving us ears to listen for them:
We thank you and bring you our praise.
For weaving dreams and letting us share them:
We thank you and bring you our praise.
For the love beyond words and telling:
We thank you and bring you our praise.

(392) Meditation

Play music with discords, e.g. Charles Ives or modern experimenters aiming to 'stretch our ears'. Then pray the following:

(393) Prayer of Petition

Lord, through discords, give us ears for your harmonies.
Where we have grown too used to what we know and like,
Challenge and change us by your warning note of love.

(394) Prayer of Dedication

Coins are here to be spent for the sake of your love;
Gifts are here to be used in the cause of your Kingdom;
Lives are here to be of service to the God of grace.

(395) Prayer of Dismissal

Go with ears open, eyes wide, hearts ready for the God who is your
life:
We go walking in his grace, to live by faith and act in love.

SUNDAY BETWEEN 20 AND 26 NOVEMBER INCLUSIVE

(Sunday before Advent)

Jeremiah 23.1–6 and Luke 1.68–79 or Jeremiah 23.1–6 and Psalm 46;
Colossians 1.11–20; Luke 23.33–43

KING OF PARADISE

Presentation

*Illustration: Objects that are not what we expect them to be, e.g. a
jack-in-the-box, a pencil case shaped like a mobile phone etc. Jesus
was a king who surprised everyone. He came to the cross. Robbers
mocked him and expected him to save himself. He reminds us today
that his Kingdom was different from all expectations. On the outside
he seemed to be an ordinary criminal, defeated. In reality, he is the
King of paradise. What things about Jesus and his Kingdom still
surprise us?*

(396) Call to Worship

Jeremiah 23.5–6 or Psalm 46.10

(397) Prayer of Adoration

Astonishing God, glorious in paradise,
We worship you, mighty King above all kings.
Working Word, from the beginning of time
You were shaping the rocks and rivers,
Planting your love in the fibre of creation.
King above all kings: **we worship and adore you!**

You put all things under Jesus' feet,
Crowning him King of earth and heaven.
You were pleased to hug all things back to your heart
With tender love for the scattered and shattered ones,
Making peace through Christ's blood on the cross.
King above all kings: **we worship and adore you!**

(398) Prayer of Confession

King and Judge, we come to you;
We could not trust anyone else to listen and care
About our daily soap opera of mistakes and crises.
This is not fiction, but our life.
This is what frightens and shames us.
We have been backbiting and gossiping: you know we have.
We have been ignoring and badmouthing: you know we have.
We have been cocky and careless: you know we have.
Silence
We can't turn off some TV to shut off our guilt.
We need to come to you, God of reality.
You are the only one who can forgive us.
Silence
Lord, we know you hear and forgive what we have told you.
Nothing can shock you or make you turn away.
Your mercy and justice are making us whole.

(399) Prayer of Dedication

On this day when we celebrate you as King,
You have shown us the way to a different Kingdom.
You said to the thief on the cross:
Today you will be with me in paradise.
Because of your kingly promise:
May our money be used with a different generosity.
May our gifts be used with a different freedom.
May our lives be used to build a different Kingdom.
May we be worthy to come home to your Kingdom to live with you.

(400) Prayer of Dismissal

Colossians 1.11–12

Appendix – Other Festivals and Special Occasions

CHURCH ANNIVERSARY

Genesis 28.10–22 or II Chronicles 7.11–16; Psalm 84 or Psalm 122;
Matthew 12.1–8 or John 4.19–26; Ephesians 2.19–22 or I Peter 2.1–5

CHRIST OUR CORNERSTONE

Presentation

Illustration: Fax or email printout with a message of congratulation to mark the number of years your church has been built. Have a telegram from the Queen on display if any member is old enough! The Queen celebrates with her subjects, as our King is central to our celebrations today. Other visual aids might include a birthday cake with symbols from your church life and candles (the light of Christ) to celebrate. The service could begin or end with a dance or procession to or from the foundation stone.

(401) Call to Worship

Psalm 84.1–2 or Psalm 122.1

(402) Prayer of Adoration

God our Builder and our Blessing,
How lovely is your dwelling place, Lord God Almighty!
Better is one day in your courts than a thousand elsewhere!
On our Church Anniversary day, our birthday festival,
We praise you, Holy Spirit, that through you
The universal church was born in flame and grace.
We worship Christ, the living stone that humankind rejected,
Now built into the fabric and foundation of all we do here in his
    name.
How lovely is your dwelling place, Lord God Almighty!
Better is one day in your courts than a thousand elsewhere!
I rejoiced with those who said to me:
Let us go to the house of the Lord!
Bless your house here at   , Lord,
And build us afresh into those living stones you created us to be.

(403) Prayer of Confession

Loving God, there are times when in your house
We have been less than living stones.
We have been dull in worship, slow in service and lax in love.
There have been times when in your house
We have rejected Christ our Cornerstone,
By not making everyone welcome, by not noticing someone's pain.
Forgive us and make your home again in our hearts.

(404) Prayer of Thanksgiving

Thank you, Living God, for the privilege
Of worshipping you in Spirit and in truth.
Thank you for the faith of Jacob and Solomon,
Who raised stone and temple
To mark a place of encounter with you,
A place to worship the one and only God.
Thank you that Jesus is greater than any temple,
Yet comes to build us up into a spiritual house for your glory.
Chosen by God, and precious,
We thank you for your presence here among us in this place.
We thank you for your presence with us wherever we wander in
    your world,
And for the people who have shared in worship here
Since the day the stones were raised.

(405) Prayer of Dedication

God, these stones were raised to your glory in former days.
We offer ourselves to be built into the living stones of the future,
Cemented together by your love, windows lit by the light of Christ,
Home for all that need to shelter with us.

(406) Prayer of Dismissal

God said: *II Chronicles 7.16*

COVENANT

Exodus 24.3–11 or Deuteronomy 29.10–15; Jeremiah 31.31–34;
Romans 12.1–2; John 15.1–10 or Mark 14.22–25

WRITTEN ON OUR HEARTS

Presentation
*Illustration: A piece of thick rope. Point out that from a distance it
seems to be a single thing. Then home in on the strands. This is what
gives it strength, holding it together and making its strength useful to
others. Our Covenant with God depends on both parties being bound
together. What happens when a relationship is one-sided? With God,
it has to be mutual, making us one with him.*

(407) Call to Worship

Romans 12.1–2 or Jeremiah 31.31–33

(408) Prayer of Adoration

God of the Covenant, who spoke to Moses on the mountain,
Reaching out to your children,
To those who stood there then and to those yet to be born:
God whose Covenant is relationship and responsibility:
We adore you.

God of the Covenant, who spoke through Jeremiah
Of a time when your law would live in the thoughts
Of your children and be written on their hearts:
God whose Covenant is binding in flesh and blood:
We adore you.

God of the Covenant, who speaks to us today,
You call us as branches in your vine, as living sacrifices.
You are our God and we were born to be your people:
God whose Covenant is now renewed between us:
We adore you.

(409) Prayer of Confession

Covenant Lord, through your servant Jeremiah you said
That you would forgive our wickedness
And remember our sins no more.
Confident in your faithful promise, we confess to you:
We have jeopardized our relationship with you,
Through neglect, through laziness, through arrogance.
Through weakness, through ignorance and through fear.
Silence
Forgive us, faithful Lord, and remember our sins no more.

(410) Prayer of Thanksgiving

Our God, we thank you: for the Covenant that binds us to one
  another.
Our God, we thank you: for the trust that you have placed in us.
Our God, we thank you: that you treat us like adults.
Our God, we thank you: for sharing the responsibilities of your
  Kingdom with us.
Our God, we thank you: for making us children of your promises.
Our God, we thank you: for bread and wine, which feeds us and
  fills us anew.

(411) Prayer of Dedication

Lord God, your people of the old covenant said:
Everything the Lord has said, we will do.
As children of the new covenant,
May we know you from the least to the greatest.
Take us as we make the ancient pledge, and do a new work in us:
Everything the Lord says, we will do!

(412) Prayer of Dismissal

Let us go, bound to our Creator by his covenant of love and promise,
bound to Christ by his covenant of responsibility and action, bound
to the Holy Spirit by the covenant of relationship and joy and bound
to one another by the privilege of living in his grace.

HARVEST THANKSGIVING

Genesis 8.15–22 or Deuteronomy 26.1–11 or Ruth 2.1–23; Psalm 65;
Matthew 6.25–33 or John 6.24–35; I Timothy 6.6–10 or
Revelation 14.14–18

REAPING THE RAINBOW

Presentation
*Illustration: Talk about the gifts on the harvest table, noting any less
common contributions like coal, water, crafts etc. that reveal the
variety of God's gifts. Nothing here was made from nothing by those
who brought it! Make a list of the most basic elements that form the
more complex items (the ore that was made into tins, the plants that
provided the textiles for crafts etc.). You will soon have a list of
reasons to thank God, as nothing has been made by humans alone.
Use the ideas generated to inform a time of prayer.*

(413) Call to Worship

Psalm 65.4

(414) Prayer of Adoration

God of the harvest, Giver of grain and good gifts,
Everything we have comes from you.
Lord of promise and plenty, you provide
From the seed to the shoot and through to the ripe fruits and pulses.
From day to night, from summer to winter, in heat and cold,
Your promise never fails.
God of the harvest, we dance with the corn and sing with the
   meadows,
Bringing you gladly the firstfruits of our worship.
God of gift and giving, today we offer you back
Tokens of your generosity, proof of your provision,
Laying them on the altar in all their rich variety.
We praise you for Jesus, the Bread of heaven.
For his sake and through the Spirit
Who pours out gifts from the fountain of God's grace,
We gather to adore our harvest Lord.

(415) Prayer of Confession

God of harvest, Bringer of hope,
Forgive us when we have closed our fists to giving,
Closed our hearts to the needs of your hungry children.
Forgive us when we have harmed your earth
Through greed for convenience.
When we have chosen comfort over caring,
God of harvest, forgive and lead us forward by your mercy.

(416) Prayer of Thanksgiving

*Use the list gathered during the presentation. Allow all ages in the
congregation to share reasons to thank God. Use drawings and
movement as well as words where appropriate. A response each time
could be:*

God who gives:
We give you our thanks and praise.

(417) Prayer of Dedication

God of the golden gifts of harvest,
God of the rainbow promise,
Take our offerings, of fragrance, craft and texture,
Our gifts and talents, our time and tastes and dreams.
All are yours. May all be used for your glory.

(418) Prayer of Dismissal

Go, content with what you have from the Father, eager to share it in
Jesus' name and on fire with the Spirit whose fruits endure.

JOHN AND CHARLES WESLEY

(For use on 24 May, or on the Sunday nearest to 24 May if it is not Pentecost)

Isaiah 12.1–6 or Isaiah 51.1–3, 7–11; Psalm 130; Mark 12.28–37 or Luke 10.1–12, 17–20; Romans 5.1–11 or II Peter 1.1–11

A BRAND PLUCKED FROM THE BURNING

Presentation

Illustration: Something saved from destruction. Tell the story of the Epworth Rectory fire that John Wesley looked back upon as God saving him for his future work. Are there personal testimonies which might be shared of looking back at life-changing events and seeing God at work in them? Read Isaiah 51.1–2. Methodism may have had small beginnings but when God blesses the work, he can draw people in. He can do so again! From a house fire to a heart 'strangely warmed', the Spirit is moving among his people!

(419) Call to Worship

Isaiah 12.2–3 or Psalm 130.1–6

(420) Prayer of Adoration

First encourage members of the congregation to look through their hymnbooks for Charles Wesley's hymns and pick out phrases that particularly express praise in ways dear to the hearts of Methodist people. Then have them read out the line they have chosen, to which the whole company will respond:

Sing to the Lord, for he has done glorious things!
Shout aloud and sing for joy!

(421) Prayer of Confession

Lord, as your Methodist people gathered in this place, we confess
That we have sometimes sung with cold hearts,
Unwarmed by your Spirit of fire.
We confess that there are many times
When we have forgotten the example of our founders,
And stifled the inspiration that led them forward for you.
Forgive us when we have closed our doors

Instead of making all the world our parish.
Forgive us when we have lost our focus on mission
And stayed at home in comfort and stagnation.
Silence
Breathe through us, heart-warming Spirit,
Strangely, urgently, reviving us with your power.

(422) Prayer of Thanksgiving

Read Luke 10.1–3

God of the church, Carer in the parish of the world,
We thank you for raising up among us those who take your words
    to heart.
Thank you for sending out your disciples
As lambs among wolves, on fire with your presence.
We thank you for the example and witness of John Wesley,
Who rode and preached in unchurched neighbourhoods,
Reaping a harvest for you through all this land.
We thank you for Charles Wesley,
Whose words enable your people to sing their faith
As they sing your praise.

(423) Prayer of Dedication

Make us worthy, God of method and mystery,
To carry on the work begun with you,
And never rest until you take us home.

(424) Prayer of Dismissal

Let us go together into all the world, which is our parish, to sing
our faith and the praise of the Creator, to do the work of Jesus
Christ and to carry the warmth of the Spirit in our hearts.

REMEMBRANCE

Psalm 9.9–20 or Psalm 46; Isaiah 25.1–9 or Isaiah 52.7–12 or
Micah 4.1–8; Matthew 5.1–12 or Matthew 5.43–48 or John 15.9–17;
Romans 8.31–35, 37–39 or Revelation 22.1–5

A STRONGHOLD IN TIMES OF TROUBLE

Presentation
*Illustration: Pelmanism, the memory game in which alternate
players pick up pairs of cards from face down until by memory they
can pick matching pairs, which they can 'capture'. (Play with a very
limited number of matched pairs, to keep the game easy and short.)
Memory is part of being human. We have a shared history, often a
very painful one. We need to be sensitive and to respect what others
can remember from conflicts all over the world, recent and more
distant. In God's family, we are to share one another's pain. Even
when we cannot remember people personally, the things they did can
still affect our own lives. As Jesus does.*

(425) Call to Worship

Psalm 46.1–2, 8–10 or Micah 4.2–3

(426) Prayer of Adoration

Almighty God of all nations, all peoples,
We gather to worship you on this Remembrance Sunday.
God who remembers: **we praise your name.**

You are the God who beats swords into ploughshares
And spears into pruning hooks.
God who remembers: **we praise your name.**

We look back with gratitude for those who have given
And continue to give their lives in the horror of war.
We look with you to a time when all warfare shall cease.
God who remembers: **we praise your name.**

God of peacemakers and peacekeeping,
Nothing can separate us from your great love
Which is in Jesus Christ.
Keep us in your peace for your own name's sake.
God who remembers: **we praise your name.**

(427) Prayer of Confession

Silence
Faithful God, in the silence of remembrance,
Memories and images crowd into our minds.
You are our stronghold in times of struggle.
At quiet times we struggle with our own consciences.
We are conscious of wrongs done and not put right,
We are aware of words spoken that we now regret,
We are conscious of decisions taken and hearts broken.
We cannot turn back the clock, but we turn to you now.
Take all the sins and grief that weigh heavily on our hearts
And wash them all in the river of your peace.

(428) Prayer of Thanksgiving

God our Rock, for opportunities to remember and for opportunities
    to forget;
For courage shown in dark hours and for resilience in times of
    peace;
For your ever-present help in times of trouble;
For your never-failing comfort in days of grief;
For the lessons of yesterday and hope for tomorrow:
We give you thanks and praise.

(429) Prayer of Dedication

May we always be peacemakers, not cowards.
May we always be bridge-builders, not warmongers.
May we always be used for you in the healing of the nations.

(430) Prayer of Dismissal

John 15.12–13

WATCH NIGHT

Deuteronomy 8.1–20 or Ecclesiastes 3.1–15; Psalm 8 or Psalm 90;
Matthew 25.31–36 or Luke 12.13–21 or Luke 12.35–40;
Revelation 21.1–6a

WAITING WITH LAMPS TRIMMED

Presentation

*Illustration: Large hourglass or egg timer. Watch the sands running
out together. Patience is needed in our Christian life. Compare
different kinds of waiting that evoke different emotions, e.g.
expecting the birth of a baby, waiting for the visit of a loved one, or
waiting for the train that is late or never turns up! What is tonight all
about? Jesus is always worth waiting for. How can we prepare our
hearts for him?*

(431) Call to Worship

Psalm 90.1–2 or Ecclesiastes 3.14–15

(432) Prayer of Adoration

God of all time and space,
In the long watches of the night: **we worship you.**
As time ticks by we watch for your signs
And rejoice at your coming to be among us.
You have been our God since before the creation of time itself.
In the long watches of the night: **we worship you.**

In the long watches of the night: **we worship you.**
With our lamps of faith trimmed
And our jars of the oil of joy in our hands,
We have come to make the bridegroom welcome.
In the long watches of the night: **we worship you.**

(433) Prayer of Confession

God of all time, Healer of your people,
We come to ask forgiveness for our failures and faults.
When we have fallen asleep over tasks with no glamour attached.
When we have run out of oil, for laziness and complacency.

When we have missed opportunities because we had run after excitement.
When we have missed the moment, because we had given up on you.
Forgive us, midnight Stranger, and let us come home to your love.

(434) Prayer of Thanksgiving

Holy God, thank you for your presence in our history:
And your love for us this night.
Thank you for company to watch with:
The sisterhood and fellowship we treasure.
Thank you for the seasons and tides of time:
The ebb and flow of our lives.
Thank you for making all things new:
Alpha and Omega, our beginning and our end.

(435) Prayer of Dedication

Ageless God, a thousand years in your sight
Are like a day that has just gone by.
Morning through to evening the grass flourishes and withers,
And we are swept away like a brief watch at night.
We do not know the day or the hour.
Find us ready at the moment of your coming,
Faces radiant with the light of Christ.

(436) Prayer of Dismissal

Revelation 21.5–6a